YOUR MAN IS WONDERFUL

How to Appreciate Your Partner,
Romance Your Differences, and
Love the One You've Got

NOELLE C. NELSON, PH.D.

Free Press
New York London Toronto Sydney

*f*P

FREE PRESS

A Division of Simon & Schuster, Inc.
1230 Avenue of the Americas
New York, NY 10020

First Free Press hardcover edition January 2009

FREE PRESS and colophon are trademarks of Simon & Schuster, Inc.

For information about special discounts for bulk purchases,
please contact Simon & Schuster Special Sales at 1-800-456-6798 or
business@simonandschuster.com

Book design by Ellen R. Sasahara

Manufactured in the United States of America

10   9   8   7   6   5   4   3   2   1

Library of Congress Cataloging-in-Publication Data
Nelson, Noelle C.
Your man is wonderful: how to appreciate your partner, romance your
differences, and love the one you've got / Noelle C. Nelson.
p. cm.
1. Man-woman relationships. 2. Interpersonal relations. 3. Men—Psychology.
I. Title.
HQ801.N45 2009
646.7'8—dc22   2008027882

ISBN-13: 978-1-4165-9350-8
ISBN-10:   1-4165-9350-0

AUTHOR'S NOTE

The examples, anecdotes, and characters in this book are drawn from my clinical work, research, and life experience with real people and events. Names and some identifying features and details have been changed.

*This book is dedicated with love and respect
to the original wonderful man, Russell.*

CONTENTS

PREFACE

I DIDN'T GROW UP WITH BROTHERS. I had a dad, a wonderful dad, but my world was filled with women for the first sixteen years of my life. I went to an all-girls' elementary school and high school, where the teachers were women, with two exceptions: the chemistry teacher and the tennis pro. It was only in college that I experienced men, but I knew them only as professors, classmates, or dates. Once again, my encounters with men were limited.

When I entered the work world, however, first as an acting coach, then as a psychologist, and then as a trial consultant, my life was flooded with men. I feel tremendously privileged that I came to know men in the workplace, discovering their vulnerabilities, fears, and insecurities, as well as their triumphs and camaraderie. Perhaps it is because I never developed any particular overriding prejudice about men as a group during my early years that I am well suited to listen to them—and they do talk to me, at length and in detail. And somewhere along the way, I discovered that men are wonderful.

This is not to say that women aren't wonderful. We are! The wonderful men you'll read about in this book are blessed with the wonderful women in their lives. This book is my response to what I see as the undeserved male bashing that exists in our culture and to the many women who have walked into my office over the years and asked, "Where are all the wonderful men?" Over my years of listening and watching, I've discovered that they're there; we just have to learn to recognize them.

Of course, there are rotten apples among men, just as there are among women. I discuss how to recognize and avoid the bad apples in the book appendix, "Men to Avoid." I also discuss this in greater detail in my previous book, *Dangerous Relationships: How to Identify and Respond to the Seven Warning Signs of a Troubled Relationship*, which is devoted to a certain type of rotten apple. This book, however, is about the discovery that inspires me: that men are wonderful, and yours can be too.

YOUR MAN IS WONDERFUL

ONCE UPON A TIME, you knew a wonderful man. Maybe it was during those first few weeks of courtship; maybe it was while you were dating; maybe it was even for that first magical year or so of living together, of marriage. Then one day you turned around, and your prince had become a toad. Instead of wonderfulness, there was too much silence, too many fights, too many lonely evenings staring at the tube.

When you talked about it with your girlfriends, they all said, "That's just the way men are: great until they've caught you, and then it's 'Get me another beer' or 'Quit nagging!' They're just not ready for lifelong romance." Heck, even our Hollywood royalty can't sustain romance. They have humongous weddings and declare their undying love, but their marriages fail within months on beds of infidelity or with lukewarm declarations of "we're too different."

So you give up. There are no wonderful men, you think, just some men you can tolerate better than others. That wonderfulness you thought you saw was just an illusion, some fancy flash dance to get you into bed or to keep you wanting him regardless of his bad behavior.

How disappointing! How hurtful! How utterly unnecessary. You see, wonderful men are everywhere, and that's what this book is about: what a wonderful man is, how to recognize one, and how your prince can remain a prince throughout your relationship, not just during the honeymoon phase.

The little-known secret is that a wonderful man is probably sitting next to you right now. Somewhere inside that boyfriend or husband or that man you just met on a blind date is a wonderful man, just waiting to reveal himself. Finding a wonderful man isn't so much about looking for him out there somewhere, a needle in an impossible haystack, as about discovering how wonderful your man is.

First things first:

What is a wonderful man?

A wonderful man is a good person. When you look around you, you'll find that most people are basically good. People are, for the most part, honest, caring, and helpful, at least when asked. There are far more good people in the world than bad. It's just that more often than not, the bad demand more attention. When we women think about men, we forget about all those good ones, focusing instead on the attention-grabbing bad apples, and declare, "All the good men are taken."

They are not. Only a few men are spectacularly rich, good-looking, and successful, as well as caring and kind, but there is no shortage of men who are good people. One of them probably is your boyfriend, your husband, or that blind date.

This is not to say that there aren't bad apples. If you meet such a man, don't get involved with him, and if you are in a relationship with one, get out. These men are easily recognizable (see the appendix for warning signs of men to avoid).

The characteristics of a wonderful man are also easily recognizable. He is:

- Basically honest
- Reliable (he does what he says he's going to do most of the time)
- Trustworthy (if he says something is so, then most likely it is so)
- Responsive (he responds to the world about him appropriately, he participates in life and doesn't just sit on the sidelines)

- Responsible (he takes responsibility for his thoughts and actions and is willingly accountable for both his successes and mistakes)
- Appreciative of other people and caring about their welfare

That's it. He doesn't need to be tall, dark, and handsome, or wealthy, stylish, and ultracool. All the other qualities you may seek—a good sense of humor, intelligence, a nice physique—are certainly important and valid, but they do not necessarily make a man wonderful.

We have trouble recognizing wonderful guys because:

1. We don't realize how important and valuable these basic qualities, the building blocks of a wonderful relationship, are.
2. We pick (to death) at a man's superficial flaws.
3. We don't provide an emotional climate in which good qualities can flourish.
4. We demand things other than what they have to offer.

This book will help you discover how good your man is and show you how to nurture his wonderfulness so that it flourishes, bringing you the heaven on earth that a relationship with a wonderful man can be.

The foundation of this knowledge is the real-world wisdom imparted by a group of women whom I call the Ladies. They come from different walks of life but share an exceptional understanding of how to nurture wonderful qualities in their men. The Ladies came together to give us their thoughts on what makes a man wonderful over the course of a series of roundtable discussions. They came from different life experiences, age groups, and ethnic backgrounds. Some have been married for decades; others are newlyweds. Their only commonality is that they all felt they were either married to or in committed relationships with wonderful men. What they had to say about their relationships, their stories, are both the inspiration and the basis for this book.

I bring to the discussion my insights and findings that come from my twenty years as a psychologist working with couples. I have shown many women the way to relationships with wonderful men, and this book is structured to guide you along that journey over the course of five weeks. At the end of each chapter, you'll find that week's "35 Days to a Wonderful Man" day-by-day guide. Each chapter builds on the one that came before, so it's best to do the thirty-five days in sequence. A "How Did I Do?" chart follows each week's guide so you can see just how well you're doing, one day at a time.

You may find that you're more comfortable working the thirty-five-day plan at a slower pace, choosing to do just a couple of items a week, and that's fine. You may find that some of the week's items are already second nature to you, and that's great. Congratulate yourself, and move on to items that may be more challenging. The best approach for you may be to read the whole book first and then begin the plan. What's important isn't that you religiously adhere to the thirty-five-day plan on that specific time line. The week's guide provides a framework within which you can develop your ability to reveal and nourish the wonderful in your man, so work at the pace at which you feel comfortable.

You can have fun with it too! Get a girlfriend to work her thirty-five-day plan with you so you can laugh, cry, or groan together over what you learn about yourselves in the process. Discovering what's wonderful in your man is a guaranteed way to find out what's wonderful in you, and sharing that with a friend can be delightful.

Maybe you're not sure that your guy really is as wonderful as I'm telling you he is. If he were, wouldn't you know it? And if his wonderful traits are hiding, why is it your job to usher them into the world?

Why can't he just wake up, smell the coffee, and be that wonderful man? He's not revealing himself as a wonderful man because, for whatever reason, you're not allowing him to. If you want the joy and fulfillment of a relationship with a wonderful man, the ball is in your court. As you read this book, you'll see that it's actually easy to reveal the wonderfulness in your man.

This plan will play out differently in your life depending at least in part on where you are in your relationship. Here are some guidelines that will allow you to adapt the plan to your relationship, whether you're dating or have been married for decades.

First Phase: You Want a Relationship with a Wonderful Man

You aren't in a relationship, but you would like to be, so you're dating. You've probably experienced some not-so-wonderful men, so you want to be in a relationship with a wonderful man.

Great! The information in the book will serve you well. Take note of the bad apples to avoid (described in the appendix) and then use the criteria in Chapter 1 to determine whether someone you're interested in is basically a good man. In brief, is he honest, reliable, trustworthy, responsive, and responsible, and does he like other people and care about the welfare of others? Don't just say, "Yeah, yeah," to this list. Pay attention to how this man leads his life, tends to his work and other interests, interacts with the people, animals, and things in his life, as well as his attitude and behavior toward the people and things on the periphery of his life: waiters, salespeople, people suffering on the other side of the globe, our planet, our environment. You will learn a great deal about the man's honesty, reliability, trustworthiness, responsiveness, responsibility, and compassion from patient and diligent observation.

As you're observing the man you're interested in for his "good guy" qualities (or lack thereof), practice what you've discovered in reading this book. Use whatever items in the thirty-five-day plan that make sense to you as you go along. Start by looking at the differences between the two of you as valuable (Chapter 1), praise what you legitimately believe is praiseworthy (Chapter 2), and practice accepting (not necessarily approving!) who this person is (Chapter 3). As you do so, notice what you're getting in return. Does this man respond by looking at the differences between you as valuable? Does he praise you to yourself and to others? Is he accepting of who you really are?

Give it time. Pretty much everyone looks and acts wonderful for the first three months of a budding relationship, sometimes referred to as "the ninety-day wonder." Don't race from practicing acceptance to embracing complete best friendship in the heady rush of the first few weeks just because you feel so utterly compatible. The proof that he's a good guy will emerge in six months, one year, and onward. Remember that you're seeking to build a lifelong relationship here, so putting in the time is well worth it.

Meanwhile, you're developing and honing your ability to reveal the wonderful within the man who eventually will be your prince as you work your way through the thirty-five-day plan. Even if it takes a few tries before you attract a good man who is for real (he makes it past the ninety days), you'll be that much readier and better able to sustain the emotional climate that allows the wonderful to emerge when he comes along.

Second Phase: You Want Your Honeymoon Bliss to Last

Let's take the next step along the relationship journey: you're in a committed relationship, either newly married or at the start of living together. You're in that glorious honeymoon phase where all's well in your world: he loves you, you love him, and what more could you ask? Well, that the honeymoon will last and last and last.

Here's where putting all the information and insights you've gleaned from working your thirty-five-day plan come into play. If you start right now, from your joyful beginning onward, to value your differences, praise your beloved, accept him fully and make it safe for him to be himself, support him enthusiastically in his desires and goals (Chapter 4), forgive him with a generous heart (Chapter 5), engage in his life and what matters to him (Chapter 6), and allow that best friendship to develop (Chapter 7), you will truly live your honeymoon all your days as your love deepens, matures, and grows.

Read the Ladies' stories for examples of how they lived their relationships, nurturing the wonderfulness in their men and letting their good qualities shine through the challenges of everyday life. Use their stories to inspire you with the knowledge that anything the Ladies can do, you can do. These Ladies are women like you and me, ordinary people, but they were able to create extraordinary relationships using the principles described in this book—and so can you.

Third Phase: You Want Your Mid- to Long-Term Relationship to Be Wonderful

Let's continue our journey down the relationship path. You're in a mid- to long-term relationship. You've had your ups and downs, but you're still together, whether out of love or habit. You're anywhere from content to mildly dissatisfied to downright unhappy, but your man is basically a good person and you want to remain in the relationship.

Mid- to Long-Term Scenario 1

Let's say you're unhappy. You're in a perfect place to use this book to get your relationship back on track. You may have to buckle down and arm yourself with a major dose of self-discipline, however. It can be a formidable challenge to make the effort to value someone's differences when you're miserable, praise him when you're feeling ignored, cheer him on when you're depressed, and forgive him when you'd rather get revenge. However, you're up to it, or you would never have picked this book up in the first place.

Follow the thirty-five-day items assiduously. Do your best not to argue with your man or engage in criticism (whether out loud or internally) as you work on these new ways of thinking and behaving. Appreciate and praise yourself for the process you're engaged in. Make notes for yourself of any positive response your man offers to what you are doing.

Since like attracts like, as you develop and nurture an emotional climate that allows the wonderfulness to reveal itself, you make it possible for your man to become, once again, the wonderful man he was when you were first together. It does require patience, however, because the trust in your relationship may be considerably eroded, and healing may need to take place for both of you.

You may find it useful to share what you are doing with your man, especially after you've been working with the concepts for a few weeks and have seen his response to your changed behavior. You may find that he becomes interested in the process himself and is willing to work on it with you. This would be terrific, for working together to reestablish what was wonderful in your union is a way of partnering, which brings you closer together.

Mid- to Long-Term Scenario 2

If your relationship is generally good but you're currently experiencing some problems or going through a rough patch, you will find this book highly useful as you go through these challenging times, whatever the nature of the challenge. Pay particular attention to the thirty-five-day-plan items, and apply your newfound understanding of yourself and how you view your man to the situation at hand, so you make it through this difficult time with your relationship deeper and stronger at the end of it.

Mid- to Long-Term Scenario 3

If you are content or even quite satisfied with your relationship, you can use this book to create an even better, stronger, and more lasting relationship. Nothing in the universe stands still. If you take your relationship for granted or don't tend to it, over time it may deteriorate, no matter how wonderful it is, just as a beautiful garden does with lack of care. As you focus on the wonderful in your man and delight in the many ways you can graciously provide an emotional environment that supports his wonderfulness, you continue to develop your relationship. As you review and remind yourself of the thirty-five-day-plan items, you make sure that your relationship grows in joy and richness, that it is true to the changing individuals you both are as you make your way through life.

The Wonderful in Him, the Wonderful in You

Working the thirty-five-day-plan week by week gives you a window into the very soul of your relationship, of how you think and feel about yourself in your relationship, about men in general, and about how you behave toward your man. More than that, it gives you a new perspective into your own amazing self.

So let's agree on something. As you go on this journey, whenever that little voice inside your head says, "Why do I have to do this?!" tell it quietly and firmly, or loudly and hysterically—whatever suits your mood: "Because I want a wonderful man in my life!" and let it be.

Okay? Good. Let's begin.

CHAPTER 1

ROMANCING YOUR DIFFERENCES

A WONDERFUL MAN is not your clone.

A wonderful man is someone who, despite the many similarities you two may share, is different from you. He does things differently than you do them. He sees things differently than you see them. He behaves differently than you would in certain situations.

A wonderful man is revealed when you value those differences, when you recognize they are part of what makes him wonderful—when, rather than resenting those differences, you come to see just how much they contribute to your happiness.

LAURIE is forty-eight years old, Caucasian, and has three children from her twenty-nine-year marriage to Jeff, also Caucasian. He's fifty-one years old, a local school administrator. She home-schooled all their children, now grown and out of the house.

Laurie: One of the things I just love about Jeff is his attention to detail. I really believe that for most of us, our greatest strength is potentially our greatest weakness. He has
that first-born perfectionism, which I've grown to adore because of what it means—that he's always looking at all the
details. When we were first married, well, it took me a while
to realize that this is wonderful.

When we were first starting our life together, he said, "I
don't like my socks folded with the cuff tucked down. Just
fold them over, no tucking." And I thought, "Okay, that's
fine." So one day sometime after that, Jeff says to me "So,
honey, why did you put my socks upside down?" I just started laughing. I said, "I guess I didn't know what was right-side
up," and he said, perfectly seriously, "The part that goes up
your legs is right-side up." That sounded so silly to me, but
I thought, "I'm going to put the socks in the drawer some
way. It doesn't really matter to me what way I put the socks
in the drawer. If it pleases him to put the socks in the drawer
that way, so be it." And there're a lot of things like that. He
had methods for things I'd never even thought of. It could
be very irritating. But as we've grown together, I've realized
I adore this man. He pays attention to all the details, which
I've learned protects me in many different ways.

For example, one day his car broke down on the freeway
on the way to work, and he was stuck there. Fortunately,
a coworker was driving by, saw who it was, and stopped
to give him a ride, so Jeff wasn't late to work. He called
me when he got to work, told me what had happened, and
said, "Honey, you're going to need to go to the car. It will
be towed, so please take my golf clubs out of the back. But
please don't park behind my car. Be sure to park in front of
it." Well, that doesn't make sense. Isn't it easier to get the

stuff transferred from his trunk to mine if I'm behind him? So I said, "Okay, but why?" And he said, "You're going to need to pick up speed to get back onto the freeway, and you can't do that if you're parked behind my car." It's little things, details, that let me know he's always thinking about me, taking care of me, protecting me.

If you look at the bigger picture, a potentially annoying difference may turn out to be a blessing.

MELIA, fifty years old, is Creole, married to Jorge, also fifty, who is Hispanic. She is the executive assistant to the managing partner of a law firm; he works in the post office. It's his second marriage, her first. They've been married twenty-one years. They have three kids, one grown and two teenagers still in the home.

Melia: As a woman who had lived on her own, I knew how to fold towels when I got married. But my husband had folded towels when he worked at a department store. He told me, "That's not how you fold towels," and I said, "What makes you the authority?" It became one of those "things," you know. I was darned if I was going to do it his way, so I just kept folding them the way I was used to. And he'd very patiently take the towels out and say, "You don't fold them that way, you fold them this way," and he'd refold them.

I don't how long it took for me to get it, but eventually I said to him, "You know what, you are the best towel folder I've ever seen. Honey, you take charge of the towel fold-ing." It was so easy! He loves to fold towels a certain way, and I couldn't care less. So why didn't I just say "Thank you so much" in the beginning? I did get there eventually, but in the beginning you are acclimating to one another; you have two different sets of eyes, two different ways of doing things, and can get hung up on the stupidest things.

If you let the little differences between you matter, they can tear your love apart. This leads you to focus on what separates you rather than on what connects you. You identify your mate increasingly with his tendencies to leave the toothpaste cap off, drop his dirty laundry on the closet floor, and forget to call when he's running late, all of which are differences you don't like, as opposed to identifying him as "the love of my life, the one who makes me laugh and hugs me when I cry." The more you focus on what you don't like, the less attention you pay to what you do like.

Our experience of life is largely a product of perception, of what we pay attention to. That's why, as studies have shown, optimists (people who see the glass half full) do better, live longer, are healthier, and are more successful than pessimists (people who see the glass half empty). They even outstrip their own talents. It's the same glass with the same amount of water in it, but what you focus on makes all the difference. Something as simple as focus has a tremendous impact on your life: better health and longer life, greater likelihood of success—and this principle applies to your relationship with your man as well. He's the same man whether you look at him with the eyes of love or with criticism; all that changes is how you focus your attention. When you pay attention to what you do like about him— the differences that you can value—you strengthen the connection between you and your man, and you strengthen the love. When you focus on what you don't like, when you see the differences between you as points of conflict, you weaken the connection between you, and the love fades.

Hurtful differences should never be ignored. If he doesn't share his feelings with you or listen to yours, for example, remember that you are an expressive person and need to be heard. If he makes major financial decisions like buying a car without discussing it with you first, this is a problem. You want and need to be involved in such decisions. But small differences, matters of individual style and preference, can bring you together as you come to appreciate them. This is what the Ladies show us: how to cherish those very differences and, in the process, make your relationship even more fulfilling.

LINDA, twenty-six years old, Caucasian, is an administrator for a local HMO. Her husband, Jack, is twenty-eight years old, Caucasian also. He is a human relations manager at a midsize company. They've been together for six years, married for three. They don't have any children. It's the first marriage for both of them.

Linda: I tend to be maybe too stingy on certain things. My husband's attitude is, "Relax, it's just money. Go get it." I tend to make too much of a deal in my head about things, and he has a way of cutting through all that. He says, "Listen, this is what it is. Just do it." So when I was worrying over what was the best advice to offer a friend who was having some financial difficulties, my husband said, "This is what you think the best advice is, right, given what you know about her?" I said, "Yes, but what if I'm wrong?" I remember he laughed and said, "Nobody can be right for everyone even half the time. Just tell her that this is your best advice and wish her well." He helps me put things in perspective. We're completely different people, but we're committed to the same team. And I have attributes in my character that he lacks. What's great is that he really wants to encourage those things in me, just like I want to encourage what's different in him, so that we can each benefit from both of our talents.

When you see a way to encourage the differences between you, you benefit from an expanded relationship.

NAOMI is forty years old and manages a small tropical plant nursery. She's half Japanese and half Caucasian, no children. Her significant other of twelve years is Buan, a second-generation Samoan American, thirty-seven years old and a U.S. Air Force pilot.

> **Naomi:** I read a story once about this lady who had a beautiful home with plush white carpets and how she loved to keep those carpets white. She would get irritated with her kids because they were always tracking mud into the house, getting her pretty carpets all dirty. Then one day, there was this awful accident, and her kids were killed. And all she did all day long after that was cry and cry, wishing with all her heart that her carpets were dirty again.
>
> That story really hit home with me. It's like, "What's important?" Those differences between me and Buan, they're what make us unique. It's easy to want only the good differences, like how he likes to drive long distances and I don't. But the other differences are just as much part of who he is, like how he's the messiest cook I know. He dirties more pots and pans than you can imagine when he prepares a meal—but you know what, it's like that woman with the carpet. I'd rather have him enjoying himself when he makes a meal than have him worrying the whole time about not making a mess. What's important? That question helps me a lot.

When you're okay with your wonderful man not being your clone, you can enjoy how he is different from you.

FLO is thirty-one years old, Caucasian, a part-time voice-over talent and full-time mom. Her husband, Andy, age thirty-three, a talent coordinator for a TV studio, is Caucasian as well. They have two children: a boy, five, and his sister, three. They've been together since high school and married for seven years.

Flo: It was funny the way I came to see my husband's differences as a good thing. I had to connect the dots. See, my best friend and I are alike in a lot of ways: we have the same basic view on life, we go to the same gym and the same church, we like the same books and movies, and we could shop for each other anytime. Imagine my surprise one day when we were talking about getting older and how to prevent getting wrinkles, and I said, "Well, I never wash my face with soap," and she exclaimed, "I always wash my face with soap!" We looked at each other in stunned silence for a moment and then burst out laughing. Ever since, when we discover something we don't have in common, we say, "Soap!" and crack up.

Well, my husband has this habit of leaving glasses around the house with just a little bit of something in the bottom: coffee, milk, soda. I'd ask him, "Please take your glass into the kitchen and rinse it out. It's harder to clean when that leftover has dried up and stuck to the bottom." He'd always say, "Sure, honey," and he'd clean up for a day or two, but then he'd forget again. I asked nicely for a while, then I nagged, then I yelled, then I gave up, and just resented the heck out of every glass I picked up. One day, I was straightening up, and I saw his glass with a gluey bit of milk at the bottom, and, I don't why, I thought, "Soap!" And I cracked up. I realized, this is no different from the soap difference with my best friend. She's a wonderful woman and a great friend. So what if we disagree about soap? My husband is a great guy, and my life is so much richer and fuller because of him. So what if he can't remember to rinse out his glass? I made a decision that day: every time I saw one of his sticky glasses, I'd let it remind me what a good man he, and that this terrific guy lives here with me—tangible proof right here in this glass! So I guess you'd say my best friend helped me see the light.

When you have what psychologists call an "Aha!" moment, you suddenly see your partner's behavior in a different light and it takes on a different meaning. What makes something significant is the meaning we attach to it. Any given situation can have a variety of meanings. For example, if your husband goes out on a Friday night with the guys, you can assign it one of these meanings:

- He's bored with the marriage.
- He's a passionate guy: passionate about being with you when you're together and passionate about being one of the guys when he's with his friends.
- He can't wait to ditch the home life and cruise the bars.
- He loves you the more for missing you one evening.
- He has some hotsie-totsie hidden away in a love nest.
- He's enrolling his pals to help him find that special piece of furniture he'll surprise you with on your anniversary.

The meaning you give to whatever is going on in your household is your choice. You can choose to see any behavior or event in any number of ways. The difference is only what you make of it—whether it's a reason to cherish or a reason to criticize is your choice.

JULIA, thirty-nine years old, is Caucasian. So is her fifty-year-old husband, Jim. This is her second marriage, his third. They dated for three years and have been married for three. She works for a landscape company, and he is a music pastor. He has three grown children from a previous marriage.

> **Julia:** We go camping a lot. I'm very reserved, especially out camping, I'm not outgoing enough to talk to people. My husband's the opposite—Jim talks to everybody. We call him "Sir Yaps-a-Lot." Not only does he ask people their name and chitchat, but he'll start talking, like to this old fishing guy, not just about his life, but about how he's been affected in his life. I mean, he really wants to know. And I like it a lot. I wish I could be like that in some ways, and yet I'm glad I'm not. It wouldn't work for me. But I admire that caring and openness in him. I respect that so much. I see the same thing in his relationships—his care for others and integrity in his relationships. He doesn't lie to his friends, pretend he is who he's not, or pretend to care when he doesn't. I always see a genuine care for his friends, for people generally, and I really admire that.

The small differences between you and your wonderful man can translate into a wide range of mutually complementary characteristics that strengthen your partnership.

MELODY is twenty-nine years old, Caucasian, and a pastor. Her husband, Patrick, a high school counselor, is twenty-eight years old, also Caucasian. It's the first marriage for both of them. They have been together for seven years, married for four, and have no children.

Melody: My husband and I are extremes in certain ways. I'm extremely organized, meticulous, punctual, detail oriented, and hard-working. I work too hard, in fact—often to the point of exhaustion. My husband is much more laid-back and carefree in many ways. Order does not have a lot of value to him, whereas it helps me rest. There's such an interesting balance between us that I didn't even know was possible. It's pacifying for me. But it does create volcanoes in other areas.

We were both getting our master's degrees, and in the process we were taking some of the same courses, but we did our assignments very differently. I would get everything done a couple of weeks ahead of time, making sure everything was handed in on time and communicating with my teacher about my grades. If I got an A-, I would find out what happened. His style was totally different: it's midnight, the assignment's due the next morning, and he's tapping away on the computer. It would stress me out to watch him do that. I would get mad at him, he would get mad at me, and our classmates would chide me to keep him on track, too, until I finally realized that if he fails his classes, it's his responsibility. I learned to tell people, "It's his problem. I can't force him to do anything." And I stopped nagging him, which allowed him to function the way he wants. I still see it as procrastination, but it's his style and I need to give him space. The same goes for him. He respects me both for doing my work responsibly and for not nagging at him. He would get frustrated when I would monitor his study habits and say, "You have five minutes." We worked it out so that now I say, "Just want to let you know that you have an eight-page paper due in a week." And then I leave it up to him. I don't drive him crazy and I don't stress about it. It gives me the ability to rest.

I've also discovered that he helps me out, too, by taking on some of my responsibilities. He says, "Don't worry. I'll take the dog to the vet. You go visit your mom." We support each other's weak areas. As I help him be more diligent, he finds opportunities for me to be more laid-back.

Our differences are good for us. We help each other improve our weak spots so we can become stronger, healthier, whole people.

Even when your differences are initially frustrating, you can find a way to work with them to both of your advantages. First acknowledge that there's more than one way to do almost anything, which is your task for Day 2 of this week's plan. You see, we each have a personality style—a way of thinking and doing that represents a constellation of traits. For example, people who are very organized also pay attention to details, plan ahead, and are usually neat and like things just so. They tend to be more reserved, both emotionally and in how they behave. People who are less organized are often more interested in impressions (taking in the whole picture) than in details and are more emotionally expressive and more spontaneous. Psychologists increasingly recognize that there are no bad personality styles, but there are certain contexts that don't work with certain personality styles. A neat, organized person will flourish in a bookkeeping position and be miserable in a seat-of-your-pants, act-on-inspiration ad copywriting position, which would delight a more spontaneous and expressive individual.

When it comes to finding the wonderful in your somewhat disorganized, frequently messy, absent-minded husband, look for the aspects of his messy personality that work for you: his spontaneity, for example, which means he'll say yes to practically anything you'd like to do at the drop of a hat; his off-the-wall ideas, dreams, and visions; his fresh food for thought and creative ways of seeing things

and approaching problems. These are wonderful traits. Yes, he forgets to call to say he'll be late to dinner, but he arrives eager to share
his funny, surprising tales of the day. Remember that that's wonderful. By appreciating his differences, you will create a context where
his personality can flourish and you will experience the joy he brings
to your life.

The same principle applies when you have a neat, often perfectionist, well-organized, everything-in-its-place husband. He makes
you feel like an idiot, for example, when he rearranges the silverware
because, as he reminds you, the little fork is supposed to be to the
left of the big fork. Yes, you knew that, but who cares? You can grind
your teeth at his perfectionism, or you can recognize that within his
orderly personality style are many valuable traits that support you:
he can balance any checkbook accurately, every time; financial goals
are easier to attain because he knows how to set small goals that
provide steps along the way; you never have to tell him where his
socks are. If you value those differences, you will create the context
that makes them work for both of you, and both of you will reap the
benefits.

LANI is fifty-one years old, as is her husband, Colin. This is a first
marriage for both and they've been married twenty-five years. They
have two children—a boy and a girl. Lani is Hawaiian Filipino and
her husband is American born of German parents. She's a homemaker about to reenter the workforce; he is a cardiologist.

> **Lani:** My husband is an M.D. and I'm a homemaker. I would
> sometimes feel threatened by that in the beginning, but we
> talked about it. He said, "Listen, Lani, you may feel threat-
> ened by my academic background, but you're more person-

able than I am. I may have a larger vocabulary than you, but you are much better at connecting with people than I am." Over time, we came to respect each other's differences and realize that we both need each other. We recognized that we make a good team because of what's different about each of us. And we even learned some of each other's skills: he's picked up on how I am able to relate to people, and he introduces me to books and other opportunities to expand my knowledge.

The more you can see how to make your differences work for you, the more valuable those differences become. Differences in education, often reflected in our choice of job or occupation, can be hurtful to a couple. The less educated person may feel intimidated by his or her partner's greater wealth of knowledge or higher position. Conflict erupts when such differences are expressed as power plays, walling each of you off into separate camps: "What do you know! You never even graduated from high school. I've got a college degree. Of course, I know what discipline is best for our children.""You're a construction worker, barely made it out of high school, and you're telling me, a lawyer, how to invest our savings?" Using your differences as a club to beat the other with denies you the great benefit such differences can afford.

A college education, for example, may provide valuable theories and techniques of child rearing, which, when combined with the practical experience of life and the collective wisdom of friends and family, add up to a well-thought-out, realistic way of disciplining the children. A lawyer's savvy combined with a construction worker's on-the-job understanding of people and how the world works, when seen as equally valuable in their different ways, can add up to a better investment plan than either partner could come up with separately.

Seeing your differences as benefits that contribute to your relationship and family life releases you from unnecessary and unhelpful conflict. It gives you the best of both worlds—yours and his.

LUCY is fifty-two years old, married for eighteen years to her husband, Jesse, who is forty-five years old. It's her third marriage, his second. She's a singer and homemaker. He's a TV cameraman for a news network. Both are Caucasian. They have two children, one still in elementary school, one in high school.

> **Lucy:** When we go to bed at night, sometimes we're so tired that we say, "I love you," just by making kissing sounds. My husband often works very late at night. Before he leaves the studio to come home, he'll always call me to say, "I'm coming home now." It could be midnight, but he thinks it's important, just like our "kiss-kiss" before we go to sleep is important. It used to kind of bug me, like, "Why are you calling me at this hour. I'm asleep!" I was grumpy one night and complained that I was already asleep when he called. He apologized and stopped doing it. After a few nights of not getting that phone call, I really missed it. It occurred to me that it was just like our "kiss-kiss"—his way of saying, "I love you and I'm thinking of you," when we're not able to go to bed at the same time at night. So I asked him to start calling me again. I said I was sorry I hadn't realized just how nice it was before. His call comforts me and makes me feel good. The phone rings, and it still wakes me up, but now I smile when I pick it up.

Understanding why your wonderful man behaves differently is often the key to appreciating those differences.

WHEN OUR MATES do things differently than we do, our first instinct often is to say, "You're doing it wrong." Obviously, we all think we're doing it right! No doubt we'd be more comfortable if our partners automatically did everything the way we do. Many of us devote considerable energy trying to persuade him to see it our way and do it our way. We don't just complain about those differences we disapprove of. For example, your mate forgets his sunglasses at the gym, and he buys a new pair rather than go without for a couple of days; he gets his morning coffee at the trendy coffee shop on his way to work instead of waiting to grab a cup at the office. We tell him we'd prefer that he was more attentive to where the money goes. We quickly escalate the criticism, telling him how wasteful his habits are, how he blows the family budget needlessly. When that doesn't work, we launch a full-scale personal attack: we tell him how selfish he is, how uncaring and unthoughtful he always is. We don't just tell him once; we repeat ourselves endlessly, hoping our nagging to will get our man to shape up.

It may even work—temporarily. Laden with the guilt you've put on him, your husband may cower and seem to accept your way as his. He may conform to your ways, usually just to get you to stop nagging. But the long-term effect on your husband, and consequently on your marriage, is devastating. Extensive research has shown that such criticism is often the beginning of a good marriage's slide into dysfunction and misery. Harping on your differences inevitably leads to bad feelings—in particular, feelings of low self-esteem. Your man can hardly maintain a healthy sense of worth when you tell him he's doing it wrong at every turn. He's only doing what is normal and natural for him. Your criticism punishes him for being himself.

Dr. Nathaniel Branden's classic work on self-esteem, *Honoring the Self*, describes what happens to people suffering from low self-esteem: they aspire to less and therefore achieve less. They seek the safety of the familiar and undemanding. They become insecure about who they are, their feelings, what they do, and as a result, they are often evasive and inappropriate in how they express themselves. To boot, they feel anxious about how others respond to them. You can readily turn a good man, with dreams and healthy ambition and the desire to create a good life with and for his family, into an insecure person with little ambition and no desire to do other than stay as safe as possible within the confines of routine, simply by repeatedly pointing out how wrong his different ways are.

Other men respond to constant criticism with hostility and anger. Although anger in and of itself isn't unhealthy, anger that results from unresolved situations leads to a marriage that feels like a battlefield, one side shooting criticism and hurtful judgments at the other at every opportunity. How can your guy possibly be wonderful in such circumstances? Whether it's about organizing socks in a drawer or the hours in the day, the bottom line is that we do things differently, and that's perfectly okay. There are almost always several equally valid points of view on how to do things.

Most people stop at this realization: "So he does things differently. I'll accept it, even though in my heart, I'm convinced my way is better." Women whose men are wonderful take it at least one step further. They recognize not just that their mate's different behaviors are okay, but that these differences are beneficial to their lives. These women value the ways in which their spouses are different from themselves. They romance those differences, meaning they come to love how their wonderful man's differences contribute positively to their lives.

Laurie, for example, has come to appreciate her husband's perfectionism as that which protects her. Many of us might just see it as a ridiculous inconvenience that we need to put up with and fault our husbands for what they see as a perfectly normal way to go about things. Laurie sees his attention to detail as his caring for her, his way to make sure she's safe and secure. She has no need or desire to change her husband's ways, which is an unfortunate tendency too many of us have. At the same time, Laurie doesn't feel the need or have any desire to become a perfectionist herself. Why should she? She likes the way she is. Laurie is comfortable with their differences and values them, and so she is able to enjoy the benefits of her husband's different ways.

Linda appreciates her husband's ability to cut to the heart of the matter when she overthinks things, whereas many women might snap, "Don't tell me what to do!" Linda understands the value of her husband's directness. She also recognizes that her husband's approach to money helps her balance out her own parsimony. She doesn't take offense, as other women might, and say, "Oh, sure, easy for you to say, 'Relax it's just money.' You're not the one who clips coupons!"

We don't always start a relationship with this ability to value and romance differences. As both Melia and Melody described, in the beginning of their relationships, their mates' differences were frustrating; Melody even experienced considerable personal turmoil from them. Yet both came to see the value of their husbands' differences. Melia happily leaves the towel folding to "the expert." Melody enjoys the respite her husband helps her find by showing her ways to be carefree and by offering to shoulder some of her responsibilities. Had either of these ladies failed to value her partner's different ways and sought to force her own approach as "the" way things must be done, neither would have reaped the benefits that very difference made possible.

Sometimes the difference isn't okay. Sometimes it requires conversation, as when Lani felt threatened by her doctor husband's ease of intellectual expression. She didn't tell him not to use big words or accuse him of condescending to her. Nor did she make herself into a talking encyclopedia in order to keep up with him. What she did was talk with her husband about it so that over time, each could respect the other's differences and recognize the contribution those very differences make to their lives.

How do you view the differences between you and your man? As a blessing or a curse? Do you attempt to make your mate do things your way? Do you impose your way as "the way we do things in our household"? Do you find yourself, for example, arguing over how the dishes should be stacked in the dishwasher, telling your mate how dumb his way is, or gritting your teeth every time he puts a plate in the "wrong" way? Often we feel we are morally superior to our men, that we know better how one should behave, and we make our mates feel subhuman because of it. But using your differences to make yourself somehow "better" than your mate will cost you dearly in closeness and stifle his ability to let his wonderfulness shine through.

Are you making your different ways something that separates you or something that brings you closer together? Because when you value your differences, that's precisely what happens: you grow closer. When your husband realizes, for example, that not only are you okay with his lighthearted conversation with the cashier as you finish doing the marketing together, but that you actually enjoy his easy banter despite the fact that you'd never do such a thing, he feels valued and valuable—and loved more.

One of the keys to happy, healthy relationships is acceptance and appreciation of difference. At the core of a wonderful man is someone who feels his different ways are valued. One of the hardest things for humans to do is accept and appreciate difference. No wonder so many of us find relationships difficult and wonderful men seem to be so rare! You can value your differences if you keep the following guidelines in mind:

1. Different is not better or worse. Different is just that—
    different.

2. People do things in different ways, go about things
    differently, approach life differently because their own
    ways work for them. These may not be the most efficient
    or "smart" or elegant ways to go about life from your
    perspective, just as how you go about life may not be
    the most efficient or "smart" or elegant ways from your
    mate's perspective.

3. Observe. Pay attention to how your mate goes about his
    life. Ask questions. Deliberately investigate how and why
    this particular approach or way of doing things works for
    him. Look for the benefits of how he goes about things.
    Seek to understand rather than judge.

4. If you want to do something together that the two of you
    do differently, figure out how your way can fit with his
    way, not how your way can replace his way. Tell him what
    you are doing and what you would like to see happen.
    Enlist his help! Wonderful men love to help. "I want to
    watch TV with you. I enjoy being with you and chatting
    about the shows," you say, "You love to channel surf. I'm
    more comfortable watching one show. How can we work
    this out together? What are your ideas?"

    When you don't make people feel wrong for having
    different preferences, they become much more willing to
    share their reasoning and open to working out solutions.
    Who wants to be cooperative with someone who makes
    angry demands or who whines and nags? No one!

5. Listen to what your mate tells you. Look more for what
    will work than for what won't. Be willing to change your
    ways, not through sacrifice but by exploring new pos-
    sibilities. Be willing to accept that there are many ways
    of going about the "doing "of life, and yours is only one
    of them. Valuing your differences will enrich your life if
    you let it.

Week #1 of Your 35 Days to a Wonderful Man: Days 1–5

This week you'll:

Stop saying, "You're doing it wrong."

Acknowledge that there's more than one way to do almost anything.

Recognize whether you view the differences between you as blessings or curses.

Stop playing "better than."

Look for what's of benefit to you in his different ways.

Day 1: Today I'll stop saying, "You're doing it wrong."

Whether you say it out loud—"Why are you doing it that way?"—with a tone that implies "you're doing it wrong," or you just think to yourself, "Boy, that's a dumb way to do that" without opening your mouth, today you will stop. When you hear yourself thinking a critical thought, zip it. Have the courage to say nothing at all, to think nothing at all, even if you have to say the words *nothing at all* to yourself over and over. You may be surprised at just how many things you think your man does "wrong." Make a note of these so you can refer to them later.

Day 2: Today I'll acknowledge that there's more than one way to do almost anything.

Today you'll observe, as you go about your day, just how many different ways there are to do any one thing. Some people put their socks on before they pull on their pants; some people put their pants on first. Socks and pants get put on either way. Some people brush their upper teeth first; some people like to start with the bottom teeth. Teeth get brushed either way. Some people get the kids up and then make breakfast; some people make breakfast and then call the kids. Kids are up and fed either way. You can squish the toothpaste tube in the middle, or you can roll it up from the bottom. You still end up with toothpaste. These may be mundane examples, but they are the stuff of everyday life. Notice all the different ways people do things yet end up with a satisfactory result. Resist the temptation to judge any one way as better than the other.

Day 3: Today I'll recognize whether I view our different ways as blessings or curses.

Today you'll identify which of your differences you think are blessings and which you decidedly label "curses." He is organized, always knows where everything is, and has a place for everything. Do you think of this as a blessing ("I can count on him to know where the stuff is that I always misplace") or as a curse ("Darn him, he's so organized; I look like a complete flake next to him")? His idea of culture is a country western concert and a rodeo. Do you think of this as a blessing ("His world expands mine; he introduces me to pursuits I never imagined") or a curse ("Spending a night at this thumping, lovelorn, 'my dog done died and my girl gone with him' excuse for music when we could be watching a good movie is ridiculous")? Don't do anything with the information yet; just notice how you label your differences: blessing or curse. Jot these down for future reference.

Day 4: Today I will stop playing "better than," as in, "I am superior to you because of how I do things."

Your ways may be more effective in some areas, and you may indeed get some things done faster or more efficiently than he does, but this does not entitle you to feel superior. Today you will refrain from putting yourself on a moral pedestal. You will cut the word *should* out of your vocabulary, at least in regard to your mate. You will make every effort to see your man as an equally valid human being as yourself, going about life in the ways that make sense to him, that have value for him.

Day 5: Today I will look for what's of benefit to me in his different ways.

Today everything you've been working on this week will come together. Now that you've stopped saying, "You're doing it wrong," acknowledged that there's more than one way to do almost anything, recognized which differences you identify as blessings or curses, and stopped playing "better than," you're ready to look for the benefits in your man's different ways. Be like a detective. Take that curse, and investigate it every which way until you can turn it into a blessing— not in a phony way, but for real. So he goes out with his buddies one night a week to play poker or watch football. He swears he'll be in by 11:00 P.M. but usually he drags in around 1:00 or 2:00 A.M. and makes his way noisily to bed. Meanwhile, you've had to cope with whatever the kids got into, did the chores by yourself, and went to bed lonely while he's out having a grand old time. Where's the blessing in that? Well, he comes back from boys' night relaxed and refreshed, and you reap the benefits of his good mood. You don't have to keep company with his buddies, which is a good thing because poker and football bore you. And you spend the evening any way you wish. Nothing says you can't hire a sitter and go see a chick flick with your best friend, sister, or aunt. You get the idea. Now do it!

Use the weekend to repeat whichever of the days were more challenging for you. Keep practicing each day's item as you go forward with your thirty-five-day plan. Don't revert to saying, "You're doing it wrong," or ignoring the blessings in your differences. On the contrary, work each day's items as much and as often as you can.

Keep track of your progress daily on your "How Did I Do Today?" chart. Enter check marks to keep track of how you did: one check for, "Yes, I did," two checks for, "Yes, I really did," or three for, "I was brilliant on this one!" and either a minus or zero if you didn't do the item. You'll be able to see at a glance how you're doing.

How Did I Do Today?

Days 1–5

Item	Day 1	Day 2	Day 3	Day 4	Day 5	SAT	SUN
Did I stop saying, "You're doing it wrong"?							
Did I acknowledge that there's more than one way to do almost anything?							
Did I recognize the differences between us as blessings or curses?							
Did I stop playing "better than"?							
Did I look for what's of genuine benefit to me in his different ways?							

Now you may find, as you work your thirty-five-day plan, that the man in your life may react to your changed behaviors and attitude in a number of ways. He may, for example, wonder why you are suddenly so understanding. Let's face it: if he's used to being ignored or constantly criticized, all this positive attention may make him uncomfortable at first. Or he may respond unappreciatively in the beginning with, "Whatever," or, "Yeah, right, anything you say, dear." Especially as you get deeper into the thirty-five-day plan over the next few weeks, your man may not immediately trust the change in your manner and ways and not react as you hope. Don't worry. Such reactions are common and normal. And don't get discouraged. Allow your man the time to get used to the new you, and just keep working the plan. If your man is a wonderful person at heart (see the Introduction for characteristics of a wonderful man), he will come to trust the changes in you. He will see that they are real, not just a passing whim, and will respond by revealing more and more of his wonderful qualities.

> Do not weep; do not wax indignant.
> Understand.
>
> SPINOZA

CHAPTER 2

BRAGGING RIGHTS

A WONDERFUL MAN is one who brags about you.

No, not brag as in, "My gal is better than yours," but brag as in he sings your praises, both to you and to others.

A wonderful man lets you know how valuable you are to him and to the world at large.

A wonderful man does not take you for granted.

Once the chase is over and you're his forevermore, he doesn't treat you like yesterday's leftovers. He isn't finished when he's won you over. If anything, you grow in value in his eyes as he discovers more and more of who you are. Time enriches his experience of you, and he loves to let you know it.

If a wonderful man is one who brags about you, he is also one you brag about.

MAY is thirty-six years old, Chinese American, a clinical pharmacist turned homemaker. Her husband of fourteen years, Tim, is also Chinese American, and thirty-three years old. He works in the legal department of a software development company. This is a first marriage for both. They have two young children.

> **May:** We got our own house, finally! And I wanted to decorate and garden and all that, even though I'd never done anything domestic before. I was a clinical pharmacist most of my life before we had kids. So when it came time to work on the garden, I told my husband not to plant any trees for me, please, because I want to plant them myself. My husband just let me do it myself. It was very gutsy, since I'd never done any gardening before. And if I made a mistake, he'd never get mad at me. At our house, we say, "If Mom plants a plant and doesn't move it at least three times, it's not our mom." I change my mind a lot. If a plant's too big for me to move, I ask my husband. So he gets out there and digs it up for me. He teases me, but he never complains. And he's very encouraging. Now that I've been a housewife for a while, when people come to visit us and they compliment our drapes or the color we painted the walls, he tells them proudly, "May did that," or, "May did all of this." He's very sweet, and he really has a lot of faith in me. Even when I do a terrible job, he gives me the opportunity to make mistakes, and he encourages me to improve on whatever it was. I appreciate him for it so much.

A wonderful man would much rather talk about your wonderfulness than point out your failings.

> **Melia:** I didn't always have healthy self-esteem, but the way my husband always lets me know he appreciates me really

helped me learn to value myself. One day I was working at the bank, and these beautiful flowers were delivered to my desk. I knew they were from my husband. He knows how much I love flowers, and that's just one of those things he does. Half an hour later, a second beautiful bouquet of flowers is delivered to me. The card said, "Because you're worth it." I just appreciate him so much for things like this. His little surprises don't need to cost money either. For years, we couldn't afford to give anything to each other. Instead, my husband would give me the sweetest notes. He works for the post office, so on the envelope, he would draw the postage stamp—with the cancellation mark! And he still does that. The other day was my fiftieth birthday, and Jorge left a hand-made birthday card on my steering wheel. I found it when I got into my car this morning. I just love that. And he does little things like that all the time, not just on special occasions.

A wonderful man never lets you forget how valuable you are.

ANNE is fifty-one years old, Caucasian, married to Tony, fifty-eight years old, also Caucasian, of Greek descent. This is her second marriage, his first. They have had three children together over the span of their seventeen-year marriage. She is a homemaker. He's a professional photographer.

Anne: My husband has become a really affectionate person. I'm not talking about just sexual stuff; I'm talking about affection. He leaves me sticky notes. There will be one on top of my laptop that says, "I love you so much," or on my steering wheel—just a random, "Don't forget I love you" or "I'm thinking about you today" inside my closet door. It's amazing! And he'll come up behind me at the least expected moments, like when I'm bent over the sink washing my face. Mascara will be running down my cheeks and I'll feel him kissing the back of my neck. I'm surprised, so I say, "Oh, honey, um, thanks, I love you too." It's so nice even if he chooses a strange moment. But what's amazing is that he wasn't very affectionate at all when we first got married. You can work with your husband and just by communicating and appreciating, you can get yourselves on the same plane. It makes such a difference to the relationship. You help one another with stress, with just getting through the day. Just knowing that I have his affection all the time really helps me out. It really calms me down and makes everyday stress easier to handle.

A wonderful man will constantly remind you of the treasure that you are.

OLIVIA is thirty-four years old, Filipino Caucasian, teaches fifth grade at a private school. In addition, she's an actress/director. Her husband, Alec, forty-one years old, is Caucasian. He heads up the customer service department for a clothing retailer. They have two kids (almost): one is four and another is on the way. They've been married five years, together ten years total. A first marriage for both.

Olivia: When my best friend and I would talk to my best friend's mom about the guys we were dating, she would say, "Yes, but do you admire him?" I think that admiration is a key to a good relationship, but it's often missing. I really admire things about my husband. He has qualities I appreciate, like how generous he is. My husband will just naturally do things for people. He's always overtipping. I'll say, "What are you doing? The service wasn't that great," but he just likes to be generous. If he's with his friends, he'll always pick up the bill. If people owe him something, most often he'll forget about it. I'll say, "So and so has your book," and he'll say. "Oh, that's okay, we'll get a new one." He just really doesn't care because he's not attached to things. He enjoys helping out, giving.

Praising your wonderful man to yourself as well as others is a delightful form of bragging.

DANIELLE is forty-eight years old, African American, has been married for twenty years to her forty-eight-year-old African American husband, Charlie. He's managing supervisor for a product distribution company. They have three children from this, the first marriage for both of them, ages seven to seventeen. She is a stay-at-home mom.

Danielle: My husband, Charlie, and I were living in Atlanta, and my parents were back in Iowa. Since our parents were getting older, we decided to move back home. It was good that we did because my dad got sick and we had to run him up to the hospital. Eventually my mom got sick too. Throughout our marriage, Charlie had a good relationship with my parents. He loved to tease my mom, and she loved to be teased by him. Eventually my mom was put in hospice, and we knew it wasn't going to be long. During one visit, Charlie walked into her room and said, "Hey, beautiful!" and he gave her a kiss. She was bedridden and in a lot of pain; I could tell that she felt anything but beautiful. I really admire the tenderness Charlie had for my mother, knowing that she thought her hair looked bad, that she looked awful and couldn't do anything for herself. He had always been very gentle with my mom, helped my parents out financially without grumbling. My dad is still living, and Charlie still helps out, without complaint. Through the years, he has always been very gentle and tender with me, always patient, and I really appreciate that. He's this way with our daughters too. If one of them is practicing the piano, he might say, "Oh, play that song again." Even with our seventeen-year-old son, he can get him to give him a hug. Most seventeen-year-olds are not into hugging their fathers. I admire that balance he has—that he's able to be strong, but he's able to be gentle too.

Looking upon your wonderful man with admiring eyes as he goes about his ordinary life is bragging.

Melody: At college, I felt I really learned a lesson in life that I hadn't learned growing up. One of my good friends at college told me about her parents, who have a really exemplary marriage, with both love and romance. I saw this firsthand when I visited with the family, even though her mom wasn't there that day. They were having company over, and my friend needed to set up for the guests. She was still setting up when the guests started arriving, so she asked her dad, "Please help me set up these chairs." And later she said to her dad, "Thank you so much; thank you for all this help with this," right in front of everybody. And even though she could tell that her dad wasn't happy that everything hadn't been set up properly before the guests arrived, once she thanked him like that in front of everybody, he smiled and was happy. I asked her, "Where did you learn how to do that?" and she said, "Well, it was modeled for me by my parents, that's how they are with each other," and I told my-self to take note of that. So if there are little things that my husband does, like he did the dishes last night, I say, "Thank you so much for doing the dishes. I'm really glad. That helps me out." Even things I expect him to do anyway—he should be helping out with the dishes and taking out the trash—I make it a point to thank him for.

Praising your wonderful man—never taking anything he does for granted—reassures him of his value to you.

JACQUI is thirty-nine years old, half African American, half Cuban, married for nine years, her second marriage. Her husband, Ron, forty-one years old, African American, was married previously, briefly. They have one child together, a seven-year-old son. She's a physician's assistant; he's a sales representative for a cruise line.

Jacqui: Even when we were dating, I always said "please" and "thank you." I naturally do that anyway, but I remember thinking, "I'm doing this on purpose."

Please and *thank you* may be little words, but their daily repetition reminds your wonderful man that you appreciate what he does for you.

Olivia: My four-year-old will be saying something about her dad, and he'll be right there in the room with us, and I'll say, "You have such a nice daddy, don't you." I say it out loud, and I'm saying it for him as well as for her.

Genuine praise enhances the experience for all concerned.

MERCEDES is thirty-two years old to her husband, Eddie's, thirty-five years of age. They are both Hispanic. This is their first marriage. They have been together a total of eleven years, married for six, and as of now have no children. They both hold administrative positions at the same company.

> **Mercedes:** My husband, Eddie, is generous with the kids we deal with in junior high. He has volunteered as their basketball coach for the past three or four years. The dad of two kids on the team passed away recently, and Eddie just stepped in and was there for the boys. He didn't try to fill the void of the boys' dad, but he was just there for them—they're teenagers. Yesterday he took the kids to a game, and they really had a good time. I think just watching him do this, really communicate with the boys, nurture them through this difficult time, shows me his sensitive side. We're not parents yet, but we hope to be, and to me it's been special to see him be so caring and good with these kids and help them cope with the loss of their dad.

When you praise how your wonderful man is with others, you support his greater value as a person.

NANCY, fifty years old, owns and operates a well-established dry-cleaning business. She's Caucasian, as is her fifty-four-year-old policeman husband, Dave. This is a first marriage for both of them. They've been married for thirty years. They have three daughters, one of whom is a special-needs child.

> **Nancy:** Sometimes you get the opportunity to see your husband differently: What does he look like in your eyes?

You can become complacent with how he behaves usually, and you start to expect rather than appreciate his efforts. Like every time my husband goes to the grocery store, I get milk and flowers. It's the nicest thing, but I don't always think to let him know how much I appreciate it.

He's a policeman so his schedule is complicated—he's gone, he's there, he's gone—but he was always there for our girls. He has coached soccer teams over the years, and he helped start a whole sports program so our daughter could play soccer and volleyball when she was young, which was quite a time commitment. He went to gymnastics meets and was the president of the cross-country track meet when our girls ran. He didn't do this because he just wanted to be the president of something—he did that for our girls. Anyway, although our daughter graduated from high school six years ago, my husband is still coaching the soccer team. I see him around young men now and how they look at him. So we were at this get-together with a number of the young men he had coached over the years. They all wanted to talk to "Coach D." I said to him, "You have such a special relationship with these young men; they still look up to you from when you coached them as boys. You've meant something in their lives." I had never looked at him like that before, but then I saw that he had a place in these boys' lives—he had mentored them.

I said to him, "You're just a magnet for these guys!" They've looked up to him, and he hasn't let them down. So many times that happens—you see some men who fall down on the job, big time. But mine didn't. I appreciate that. A lot.

When you let your wonderful man see his worth reflected through your eyes, you become a loving witness to the good he does in the world.

LYNN, forty-six years old, Caucasian, has been married for ten years to her forty-two-year-old husband, Steve, also Caucasian. They have been together, however, for over twenty years. Both of them work in the entertainment industry, in production. They have no children. This is a first marriage for both.

Lynn: My husband and I have been together twenty years. It was the '80s, and we met on a blind date. He came home with me that night and never left. We married eleven years to the day after we met. He was a bad boy, and I fell in love with the bad boy, truly, at first sight. I thought, "This is it!" It was such an overwhelming feeling. And we had ten very tempestuous years. We lived a life of sex, drugs, and rock and roll working in the production end of Hollywood. It was sad. But we stayed together the whole time, both of us drawn to the drama of our relationship more than anything else.

Well, after those first ten years together, my mother got sick, so we left our party lifestyle and our great Hollywood Hills condo to move in with her and help her out. We did this also in part because it was time to grow up and save money. I was working at the time, and my husband was not, so he spent a lot of time with Mom and saw a lot more of what was going on with her. He said, "There's something wrong with your mother," and I said, "What do you mean?" because she'd always been somewhat eccentric. He said, "Well, we've been living here a couple of weeks, and I've been noticing these odd things, like she turns the water on in the sink and walks away. She'll leave for a walk, and then I'll have to go out and find her because she can't find her way back to the house. Or she'll want to go out of the house without getting dressed."

I said, "She is kind of eccentric."

But then he said, "She was giving away money at the ATM today."

My mother was notoriously thrifty and she would never do that.

Shortly after, she was diagnosed with Alzheimer's, and my husband, still my boyfriend at the time, was the one who took care of her every day. Sometimes he would get upset or panicked—he had all the emotions of an inexperienced caretaker—but he really had what it took to be there for her. I was so incredibly grateful.

When we got married, my mother was still well enough to attend and even have her sense of humor. When we cut the cake, she wanted the first piece. And my husband gave her the first piece of cake. This small act of kindness showed me that he'd stopped being a self-centered bad boy. Even though our first ten years together were crazy, I knew at our wedding that the next ten years would be better, because my man was finally really beginning to grow up.

There were still some rough times after that, but all the while he was my mom's primary caretaker, to the point that she recognized him well after she no longer recognized me or the rest of the immediate family. I thought that was so special, and I appreciated every single thing he did for her. We weren't perfect, but his caring for my mom showed me the potential for a really good man.

And I decided to create space for him to encourage the best in him. I set my heart to appreciating every nice thing that he did for me. When he did something, even if it was something I didn't like, I would say, "Thank you." I realized that when he would do something, he would look at me as if to say, "Is she happy?" And I learned to reply, "Honey, that's so nice, you made me so happy. Thank you very much." It's grown to the point that my husband brings me the paper and my coffee in bed every morning. I had to learn to let him do things for me and to say thank you, and in return he blossomed into this incredibly wonderful guy.

Praise has a phenomenal way of nurturing the wonderful within us, even if that wonderfulness is at first hard to find.

Laurie: My husband and I had two little girls. One of them loved gymnastics, and the other daughter was into ballet— she is now a professional ballet dancer. My husband spent many years going to gymnastics and ballet events while other dads went to football games. What amazed me is that he would always find something specific to say about the kids' performances. He wouldn't just say, "You did great, sweetie." He'd say something like, "I just loved the way you did the dismount out of your flip," or, "I noticed when you were leaping across the room that your leg was extended so nicely." He'd remember the names of their moves, their teammates, whatever. His attention to detail and a tenderness said, "I care enough to enter your world and I'm going to make it more beautiful for you." It was very special to me.

The source of genuine praise is in the careful observation of the little things your wonderful man does.

Linda: You have to make a conscious decision to say thank you. I'd always thought to myself, "Gosh, Jack knows he's smart," or, "He knows he does that so well," but I've learned that it's important to say out loud to Jack, "You did a really good job with that," or, "You're so good at organizing things." It's important to him to hear how much I appreciate who he is and what he does. And maybe he doesn't know it as much as I think he does.

Praise is an attitude, a state of mind consciously chosen to honor the wonderful qualities in your man.

Mercedes: I appreciate the fact that my husband is the cook in the family. I help out, but I'm still thankful. I'm always bragging to everybody about his barbecued steaks or what have you.

Appreciation of all your wonderful man is and does is best spread far and wide.

Olivia: I hate doing dishes. I'd rather scrub a toilet with a toothbrush. And my husband loves it—it's like Zen for him. He gets in there with the soap and the water, and he's a happy man. I'm so appreciative of that! He'll come home, change his clothes, and go right to the sink, where a whole day's worth of dishes are piled sky-high. Boy, do I let him know how thankful I am for that!

The less you take for granted, the more you can enjoy your wonderful man and make life enjoyable for him.

IN COURTSHIP, we're great appreciators. We tell our new love everything that we like about him. We notice his every word or deed with applause and delight, and we bore our friends with enthusiastic descriptions of everything about the man and expect equally glowing praise from them in return. But once we get hitched (legally or otherwise), appreciation seems to go out the window. The romantic fallacy too often adopted by both sexes is, "Once won, forever conquered"— and yet nothing could be further from the truth.

You go to the nursery and walk slowly down the rows, carefully looking at every plant. Finally you pick one out: it's perfect in every regard. Once you get home, you don't stick your plant in any old place and forget about it. You know it can't thrive without sunlight and water. You put your new plant in a special place, where the sunlight hits it just right, and you water and tend to it so it can flourish. You don't expect your car to run without oil or gasoline, whether it's ten years old or the latest model. Yet we expect our mates to thrive on the merest crumb of appreciation, which we dole out on only very special occasions—or, worse, when we want something. The open expression of your appreciation, the praise and gratitude you offer him, is the sunlight and water, the gasoline and oil, of a good relationship. And a wonderful man knows this. He showers his mate with sincere expressions of how much he values her and is not shy in letting the world know how he feels.

Praise, both public and private, breeds high levels of satisfaction and fulfillment in a relationship. Why? Because appreciating your mate, singing his praise, is the end of a series of highly desirable behaviors:

- I notice who you are and what you do. I pay attention to you.
- I see value in who you are and what you do. I think well of you.
- I am impressed, uplifted, touched, or in other ways positively affected by who you are and what you do.
- I enjoy your value so much that I want to express it openly.
- I enjoy your value so much that I want to share it with others.

What a list! When you praise your man, you're telling him all this. It can be as free-flowing as you want, and it costs nothing. It's an unlimited resource. And as long as the praise is genuine, meaningful, and straight from the heart, it is fulfilling.

Appreciation is like a boomerang. When you send it out, it comes back to you. Much research on appreciation has been done in the workplace, and it shows that when employees are appreciated and given honest praise, their performance and productivity soar. A company that appreciates its employees will see triple the return of a company that fails to appreciate its employees effectively. Companies that earn a place on the coveted Best Places to Work list are filled with managers who appreciate their employees and employees who go the extra mile for their company at every turn. The reverse is also true. U.S. Department of Labor data show that the number one reason employees quit their jobs isn't lack of adequate pay but lack of appreciation.

It's no different in relationships. When you don't appreciate people, they go away, either physically or emotionally. In an extensive survey done by Lynn Gigy, Ph.D., and Joan Kelly, Ph.D., of the Divorce Mediation Project in Corte Madera, California, fully 80 percent of divorced men and women gave as one of the primary reasons for the breakup the fact that they did not feel loved or appreciated. Fortunately, appreciating others fosters within them an appreciation for you. What you give is truly what you get. As you learn to express your sincere gratitude for all that you value about your mate, he will become increasingly appreciative of you.

Take the appreciation challenge! In addition to following the guidelines for Week 2 of the thirty-five-day plan at the end of this chapter, say three appreciative things a day to your partner every day for twenty-one days (which is how long it takes to form a habit). You might say:

"It feels so good to wake up beside you."

"You look so nice, all spruced up for the day."

"Thanks for helping get the kids out the door."

"You make a great cup of coffee. Thanks."

"I love coming home to you."

"You put a smile on my face when I see you at the door."

"You're so good around the kitchen. Thank you."

"It feels wonderful to sit beside you while we watch TV."

"Mmm, your hugs are so special!"

"I feel good just being around you."

"You give me such good advice."

"What a comfort you are to me."

You will find that as you appreciate your man with these and other words of heartfelt praise, he will begin to show his appreciation for you more and more. He may not always do it in words, for many men aren't as comfortable with voicing their appreciation as we are, but by his manner and behavior, you will see a shift in his behavior. He may spend more time with you. He may ask your opinion more often. He may help out more around the house. He may become more affectionate. In one way or another, your appreciation of him will set off a corresponding appreciation for you.

Sometimes we fail to sing our mate's praises because we think, "Well, he's supposed to do this or that. After all I do . . ." and off you go on the monumental list of tasks and responsibilities you take care of. We figure our men are supposed to contribute to the relationship or to the family, so why should we thank them at every turn? But studies of the workplace have shown that people rarely are willing to work just for a paycheck, and managers who insist that employees should will end up with high employee turnover and poor productivity. So too in your relationship. Yes, it may be that we should all undertake our responsibilities even without getting that dose of praise, but the reality is that people thrive in the presence of appreciation and wither in its absence.

Appreciate your man. Shower him with gratitude liberally and often. Take nothing he does for granted, and you'll find yourself amply rewarded with more and more love. No man can be badgered, clubbed, or argued into being wonderful. Too often we criticize our men in our attempt to get them to be wonderful. It's as if we think that by criticizing the stuff we don't like, we will end up with only the good stuff. It doesn't work that way.

Here's a little-known secret about men: the vast majority of them want to please us. They want to be our knights in shining armor. They want to be there for us. They want to see the smile on our faces that tells them they are worthy.

When we ignore their efforts and fail to let them know the many ways in which they please us, they get discouraged, as would anyone, and think, "There's no pleasing her." With that, many men withdraw. And since men are often less vocal than we are, they don't tell us in words what's going on. They may not be that conscious of it themselves; the only evidence is that they are no longer eager to run to our aid, care for us, and respond to our needs.

Anything you focus on grows. If you focus on his flaws, his flaws will reveal themselves more and more. If you focus instead on his good qualities—those things he does or says that please and impress you—those qualities will reveal themselves more and more. So be quicker to spot his qualities than his flaws.

When May's husband doesn't object to her somewhat unusual style of planting trees, she recognizes that he doesn't necessarily have to be okay with her improvisational gardening. She is grateful that he is willing to let her landscape the way she chooses, to make mistakes and repot as often as she wishes, and she notices and praises his lack of complaining and even gentle encouragement. Similarly, Melia is thrilled every time she receives one of her husband's hand-made cards. Another woman might deride Jorge's hand-drawn post-age stamp as childish or say, "Why couldn't he spring for the postage? Aren't I worth a few cents?" But Melia appreciates the thought and love that go into these gifts. And that he's offered them to her on many occasions in their twenty-one years together hasn't made them any less special.

So too when Anne's husband kisses the back of her neck when she's washing her face, Anne doesn't push him aside with a perfunctory, "Not now!" or snap, "Can't you see that I'm busy?" She realizes that her husband's spontaneous affection is a gift and responds affectionately in return. Olivia praises her husband's generosity in giving to others, whereas another woman might object, wanting him to save his dollars, and she is grateful when he does the dishes after she's taken care of the kids and the house all day. Mercedes brags to everyone about her husband's cooking, letting him know in no uncertain terms how much she appreciates it, while another woman might complain that he always barbecues; why can't he sauté instead? When Lynn's husband cooks her breakfast, she doesn't say, "Yeah, fine, thanks" offhandedly, given that he has cooked her eggs the same way for years. She says, "Wonderful, absolutely wonderful," every time, because she is knows how important her sincere appreciation is to her man.

Many times, we don't realize or see these intangible gifts our men offer us. These gifts aren't obvious and showy like diamond rings, cars, and new dresses, and men don't verbally point out when they're giving us an intangible gift. ("Hey, honey, look how I'm paying attention to how our daughter executes her gymnastics routine." Hardly!) As a result, we may not receive those gifts at all, or we take them for granted, or we want something bigger and better than the gifts they offer. Or we recognize the gift but don't approve of how our man offers it: "Why does he have to draw a card? Can't he just buy one like everybody else?" In one way or another, we reject the gift—and with it, the man.

When you reject something often enough, you'll stop receiving it, and then you wonder why your man isn't wonderful. Simply put, you aren't making it possible for him to be so!

It's easy to recognize a tangible gift. What is an intangible gift?

- When he reaches over to you first thing in the morning and says, "Hi, hon"
- When he picks up the dishtowel you dropped
- When he reminds you for the third time of that appointment you made
- When he asks if you want him to pick up the kids today
- When he's buried in work and still chats with your mom
- When he says, "I love you," before hanging up the phone
- His smile when he sees you walk through the door

The list could go on forever. Intangible gifts are limitless, infinite. They cease their gentle flow only if you fail to receive them.

Deliberately make yourself aware of and appreciative of these gifts. Sing his praises! Appreciate what he says and does as often as you can, in words that you mean and in a voice he can hear.

Recognize that the way your mate delivers his gifts may not be precisely the way you'd like them delivered, but they are gifts nonetheless—for example:

- He makes your birthday plans at the last minute, so your dinner reservations are for 9:30 P.M. when you're used to dining at 6:30 P.M. Don't make both of you miserable by pointing out your growling stomach and heaving great sighs of disappointment at the late hour. Praise the thought that went into choosing a restaurant and making the reservation.

- He proudly presents you with a travel perfume holder that is woefully inadequate and hard to fill. Instead of criticizing the gift, appreciate that he noticed how much you enjoy perfume and how attentive he was to your many complaints about the lack of portable perfume bottles.

- He spontaneously brings home a fern and lovingly explains that it's a bouquet that will last longer since it's in a pot. Resist the temptation to tell him that anything in a pot doesn't qualify as a bouquet and that he should know by now that yellow roses are your idea of flowers. Appreciate his spontaneous gift! Express your gratitude at his thoughtfulness in giving you something that will last longer than a few days.

In other words, don't emasculate your mate for what he doesn't do correctly, according to your highly personalized guidelines. Instead, look for the value in all his gifts, and enjoy the wonderfulness he discloses to you with them.

And don't just appreciate what your man does for you: observe and praise what he does for others. Make your praise known to both your man and others. After all, it's not just, "You and me, babe." He exists in the larger world, and what he has to offer to that world also deserves to be acknowledged and praised. It is part of what makes him a wonderful man.

Danielle was deeply moved by her husband's tenderness toward her dying mother, a tenderness another woman might not even have noticed, or might even have resented. When Olivia's four-year-old says something nice about her daddy, Olivia responds in a way that both reinforces her daughter's good feelings and lets her husband know how much she appreciates his being a "nice daddy." Nancy was pleased that her husband took some kids who had recently lost their dad to a game and didn't accuse him of neglecting his own family.

She saw the hero in what he did, the shining knight in him. And she pointed out to her husband how the young men he had coached over the years looked up to him and didn't complain that he should have been helping around the house instead. When Lynn's boyfriend cared for her mother with Alzheimer's, she could have resented every good thing her boyfriend did for her mom, because he certainly hadn't been behaving as well toward her. Imagine how differently things would have turned out if she had grown angry at him for caring for her mom and said, "Well, you never did that for me!" Instead, Lynn made a conscious, concerted effort to appreciate every single thing he did for her mom, as hard as it must have been for her on many occasions.

Realize that you don't appreciate and praise in order to get someone to do something. Contrary to popular belief, nobody—male or female—can be molded into something they are not, at least not for any length of time. Appreciation is not manipulation. You appreciate and praise for the pleasure of doing so, as part of loving your mate, which in turn creates a general climate of appreciation. You value specific behaviors that are genuinely meaningful and valuable to you. And that climate of appreciation brings out the best in people, as both science and common sense have shown repeatedly.

You don't praise him for taking out the trash in order to manipulate him into taking the trash out again next week. He's not a dolphin you train to jump on cue. We all know and feel the difference between sincere and insincere expressions. Sincere ones hit the mark; insincere ones don't. Just in case you think a man can be fooled, here's the tale of "Six-Carat Cindy," as told by one of the Ladies:

There was a young woman who met a man, a very wealthy man. She was stunning. He was divorced. It was love at first sight for them, or lust—well, more on his part that hers, because he sort of looked like a troll. She was used to wealthy men falling all over her and spoiling her because she was stunning. Early in the relationship, he moved her into a house in a very upscale neighborhood, gave her the name of his decorator, and let her do whatever she wanted. She wasn't a bad person—in fact, she was very nice—so I knew she wasn't out to take horrible advantage of him.

I remember she drove up in a new Mercedes, and I thought, "Gee, that's a nice car. I didn't know she could afford that." Well, her man had given it to her as a gift. And I said, "Wow, I'm impressed. What did you do to get that?" and she said, "Nothing, I just said thank you." I said, "What do you mean, you just said thank you?" She said, "Every time he does something nice for me, whether he gives me one flower or money for shopping or a diamond bracelet, I take his face in my hands and say, 'Darling, thank you so much. You have made me so happy." And now he had given her a Mercedes. I thought, "Wow, this is like gold. This woman has it down pat." Shortly afterward, he asked her to marry him. We called her Six-Carat Cindy because her engagement ring was a four-carat marquis and two one-carat baguettes. We were all like, "Does that come with sunglasses and a bodyguard?"

Now, I think she really meant her thank-yous in the beginning. But sometime along the way, she lost her sincerity. She kept saying and doing the same things, but she lost the honesty of her heart. She no longer truly meant every "thank you," and he figured it out. Their relationship changed because she took for granted what he did for her. I think when she stopped appreciating him, he stopped doing things for her. And that was the end of everything. Even though they had a child together, they got divorced.

Appreciation must be genuine, but it also can be learned. As Lynn watched her boyfriend graciously care for her mom with Alzheimer's, she saw his good qualities and believed that there were more waiting to emerge. She deliberately created a space for him that would encourage him to be the very best that he could be. She taught herself to say "thank you," to acknowledge everything he did that made her happy and pleased her.

Melody discovered the amazing power of appreciation when she observed a friend thanking her dad profusely, publicly, for helping to set up chairs, and witnessed the dad's grateful response. Melody then learned to thank her husband for whatever he did around the house, even if it was something she expected him to do. Often we think that a certain chore is his duty, and so there's no need for thanks. Yet remembering to be grateful for whatever your mate does, expected or not, goes a long way toward creating a loving relationship. We are the most important people in our mate's life. When we take the time and make the effort to let our men know their value to us, their self-confidence grows, and with it, the desire and ability to be the very best of themselves.

As you truthfully appreciate from your heart your man's specific behaviors, you establish a general climate of appreciation for your mate. People flourish in such an environment. Under these conditions, your man will reveal his wonderfulness to you over and over again.

Week #2 of Your 35 Days to a Wonderful Man: Days 6–10

This week you'll:

- Revive what you appreciated about your man when you first met him.
- Express your appreciation for what you value about your man.
- Recognize the gifts, tangible and intangible, your man gives you.
- Praise the perfection of those gifts and ignore the imperfections.
- Acknowledge and praise your man's generosity toward others.

Day 6: Today I'll revive what I appreciated about my man when I first met him.

Today you'll think back to what it was like when you were first seeing each other. Remember what you liked so much about your man. Start with the physical. What was it about his physical self that pleased you? His hair, perhaps, or his size, his smile, the sparkle in his eyes? Let your memory drift back to those first times you touched: the way he held your hand, or put his arm around your waist, or that delicious first kiss.

Then turn your thoughts to what attracted you emotionally and mentally: how he made you laugh, how you admired his dedication to his work, how much you enjoyed talking about a movie you'd just seen. Reflect on the spiritual dimensions of your budding relationship, whatever those might have been for you. Resist the temptation to think, "But he's not like that anymore!" Focus only on what you appreciated about him, what you valued about him back then.

Day 7: Today I'll express my appreciation for what I value about my man.

Today you'll look at your man solely in terms of what you value about him. The memories you revived yesterday have primed you for today's exercise, as you now have brought to mind qualities that you've ignored or taken for granted as the years have gone by. Today, say, for example, "Thanks, hon, for always supporting me, for being there for me," even if your man hasn't done anything in particular for you today. You are expressing your appreciation for something he is or does in general, as part of his being. You can say, "Thanks for being so good with the kids; that's always meant a lot to me," even if the kids aren't around today. You can say, "You're such a good people person. I really value that in you," even if he hasn't interacted with anyone other than you and the dog today. Say, "I love the way you look and smell and feel" if that's true for you. As long as you are honest and genuinely appreciate a quality of your man, say it. If you've lost the habit of expressing appreciation for your man, this may be difficult, and you may be able to say only one or two things. That's okay. You've started the process. You'll get better at it as you practice, day after day.

Day 8: Today I'll recognize the gifts, tangible and intangible, my man gives me.

Today you'll deliberately recognize the many gifts your man gives you, starting with the tangible—those things that are physical. For example, your man may take responsibility for part or all of the rent or mortgage, or he may provide some or a lot of the money that goes toward family expenses. He may have bought you an outfit for your last birthday or picked up a CD he thought you'd like. He may pick up the tab for your dinners out or pay for tickets at the movies. Look around your home, and remind yourself of all the physical contributions your man has made to you, your home, and your well-being.

Next, focus on the intangible—those gifts your man gives you that are less physical (you can't taste, touch, or smell them) but are valuable nonetheless. He may remind you of an important appointment he knows you don't want you to forget, he may cook dinner for you, or he may bring you a cup of coffee first thing in the morning. He may greet you with a hug when you come home from your day, he may boast to the neighbor about how beautiful the roses you planted are, he may change the oil in your car, or he may tell you your apple pie is the best. All of these are gifts. Think through your day, your week, the past month, and write down all the gifts, tangible and intangible, that your man has given you in that brief span of time.

Day 9: Today I'll praise the perfection of those gifts and ignore the imperfections.

Having recognized the many gifts your man gives you, today you will praise those gifts, first to yourself and then to your man. The challenge for you is to ignore that voice in your head that says, "What do you mean, thank him for pitching in with the rent! So do I, and nobody thanks me for that!" or, "So he changes the oil in my car. You want a list of everything I do for him I never get any thanks for?" Thank him anyway. Tell him how much you appreciate what he is and does. Express your gratitude in words, hugs, kisses, little notes or cards—whatever makes sense for you. Be truthful. If you can't bring yourself to say, "Thanks for kicking in for groceries," don't say it. Find a gift you can appreciate, and express your heartfelt thanks for that gift: "I love that you hug me when I come home. Thank you." Don't express gratitude for something you aren't grateful for. Find what is of value to you within what he offered, and appreciate that. So when you hear that annoying voice in your head—"Yeah, sure, he bought me an outfit, but boy what an awful color!"—agree with it. That's your truth! But don't let it stop you from appreciating what you can value: "Thank you for giving me such a generous gift for my birthday." Acknowledge that you appreciate his thinking of you and what's important to you. The fact that the dress is the wrong color is irrelevant. Praise the perfection of his gifts—the part that is valuable to you—with sincerity and joy.

Day 10: Today I'll acknowledge and praise my man's generosity toward others.

It's easy to feel jealous of the attention your man gives to others, especially if you're feeling deprived yourself. That's why it's important to work your way up to Day 10. First, you need to acknowledge the abundance of gifts, seen and unseen, that your man gives to you before you attempt to praise his generosity toward others. When you praise your man for his gifts to others, be sure to include what it means to you. He wants to be *your* knight in shining armor, so it matters to him what you think of his actions. "I really appreciate the time you put into coaching soccer for the kids" is great. "I really appreciate the time you put into coaching soccer for the kids—I love what a great mentor you are to them and how the kids look up to you," is better.

Praise your man's generosity to others whether or not he's within earshot. Don't keep your gratitude to yourself; let everyone know how much you value what your man offers the world at large. This may feel awkward, especially if you're not a particularly effusive person, but it will get easier as you continue to do it.

Use the weekend to repeat whichever of the days was more challenging for you.

Keep track of your progress daily on your "How Did I Do Today?" chart. Enter check marks to keep track of how you did: one check for "Yes, I did," two checks for "Yes, I really did," or three for "I was brilliant on this one!" and either a minus or a zero if you didn't do the item. You'll be able to see at a glance how you're doing.

Remember to keep practicing the past week's items as you go forward with this week's plan.

How Did I Do Today?

Days 6–10

Item	Day 6	Day 7	Day 8	Day 9	Day 10	SAT	SUN
Did I revive what I appreciated about my man when I first met him?							
Did I express my appreciation for what I value about my man?							
Did I recognize the gifts, tangible and intangible, my man gives me?							
Did I praise the perfection of those gifts and ignore the imperfections?							
Did I acknowledge and praise my man's generosity toward others?							

Praise is like sunlight to the human spirit:
we cannot flower and grow without it.

JESSE LAIR, *inspirational author*

CHAPTER 3

ACCEPTING HIM, ACCEPTING YOU

A WONDERFUL MAN accepts you, just the way you are.

A wonderful man doesn't demand that you fit some preconceived notion he has of how a woman should be. He doesn't try to shape you into someone you're not or force the round peg that you are into the square hole of his feminine ideal.

A wonderful man likes the person you are. He is sufficiently mature to have compassion for your flaws and foibles. He does not shame or disrespect you—to yourself or to others. A wonderful man makes you feel good about yourself.

Melody: I was dating someone before I met my husband, and if I didn't always look perfect, he would notice. He was meticulous. He'd say things like, "How come you're not wearing mascara today?" or he'd suggest that I wear a different dress. How I looked was extremely important to him—more important than how I felt that day, like if I wanted to be more relaxed and didn't want to put on makeup, or if I was in a funky mood and wasn't up for wearing a dress that day. I felt I always had to dress the way he wanted.

My husband's not like that at all. He barely notices what I'm wearing. Sometimes I want him to notice, but I recognize that I appreciate being accepted even more. Even if I see in the mirror that my hair is totally messed up and I ask, "Why didn't you tell me my hair was a mess?" he'll say, "Well, I thought it looked great!" I appreciate that. I appreciate that I don't have to look perfect—or be perfect in any way—for him to love me.

A wonderful man really does love you just the way you are.

Danielle: Before we got married, I'd had a lot of problems, and some not-so-good things happened in my life. I brought a lot of baggage into our marriage, and it took a while before I could talk about it. When I finally poured my heart out to him, he looked at me and said, "You're pure in my eyes." Then I realized, "I think I could spend a lifetime with this man."

A wonderful man accepts the whole of you, including your past, innocent or otherwise.

Danielle: One thing that stands out is my husband's acceptance of me—my failures and my flaws. We've been married twenty years, and we have three children. Early on, he used to tell me all the time, "I'm not the enemy!" Once I realized that there are differences in personality and that those differences are good, I understood that he accepted me for who I am, and I came to accept him for who he is as well.

Our church in Atlanta had a Wednesday night supper, and we would go most weeks. Often my husband would go directly from work, and I'd arrive separately from the house with the kids. Well, there was torrential rain one particular Wednesday, and even though the church had just done some landscaping, they hadn't put up any cones or anything. When I pulled into a parking space, I backed into this load of newly dug earth, which was now mud. I tried to drive forward to pull the car out of the mud, but the more I tried to get out, the deeper into the mud I went. My husband walked up with his umbrella and saw the car down to the axle in the mud. He told me to go on into the church and get out of the rain, and he called AAA. Everyone who passed him on their way into the church rolled their eyes at his predicament, surely thinking, "What a dumb thing to do," and the worst, my husband said, was when the AAA guy arrived. He gave him a look that said, "I can't believe you did this." Everything in him wanted to say, "It wasn't me! It was my wife!" but he didn't. He didn't say anything. He bore my shame. He said it was fine; he just took it in. And he really meant it. I really appreciate that. And I've seen that throughout the years. He doesn't go around and tell everybody what I do wrong or bad-mouth me to anybody. It's a blessing.

A wonderful man accepts your all-too-human slipups without shaming you in any way.

Olivia: I could care less about wearing negligees and all that kind of stuff, and so I appreciate that Alec doesn't care either. When we were dating, I would say, "You really don't care? You really don't care if I just wear a T-shirt to bed?" and he'd say, "Well, no. It comes off, so it's all the same." And I thought, "Yes! That's the way I think, too." I appreciate that.

A wonderful man accepts you the way you like to be.

Lani: My body has changed over time, and I haven't kept my shape from my younger years. My husband accepts me and doesn't pressure me to be anything or anyone other than who I am. He worries sometimes about my health since I've put on weight, and he'll talk to me about that, but once I say, "Don't pressure me," he won't, and he'll say, "Honey, I love you just the way you are." I just love that. I don't feel any pressure to be this A+ wife or this perfect-looking or -performing wife. He accepts me with my frailties, just the way that I am.

A wonderful man will be straight with you but will also always accept you.

CORINNE is forty-two years old, Caucasian. This is her second marriage, as it is for her husband, Jordan. He's proudly Hispanic Caucasian, forty-three years old. He has a grown child from his previous marriage; he and Corinne have an eighteen-month-old child together. She handles the front office for a medical practice; he runs the shipping department of a midsize company. They've been married now for six years.

Corinne: I came out of an abusive relationship—my first marriage. When I married my second husband, I had to remember I was no longer married to that first, abusive husband. My second husband was not that same person as my first husband, and so it wasn't right that I would sometimes respond as I had to my first husband. I realized that I had to stop this. I told myself, "Okay, I need to learn to react the right way." My husband helped me so much with that because he loved me just as I was. I remember one time I was really upset and angry, and instead of yelling back at me or hitting me, like my abusive husband would have, he just grabbed me and hugged me, and I broke! I cried and cried from the depths of my soul and he said, "Oh, my God, what happened?" It was just the way that he held me. I was so used to being pushed away, so for him not to yell at me or anything, but to just hold me like that, I thought, "Wow, he must really love me. This man accepts me, even when I'm upset." I was blown away that he could see me for me, not get stuck on my anger or our disagreements.

What I learned from my husband is that looking at the heart of someone, who that person really is inside, will help you appreciate somebody and help you overlook those rough edges.

A wonderful man can see beyond your immediate emotions and accept who you really are.

Julia: My husband and I have never had an argument in the three and a half years we've been married in which we've raised our voices at one another. We've discussed it. I came from an abusive first marriage. I was physically abused and very scared all the time, and that ended, and I met this wonderful man, my husband. I've been at both ends of the spectrum in my life. We talk about this line of respect toward one another, this line that I can see. Why would either of us ever cross that line?

Communication is huge in our marriage. We make sure we always know where are we relative to that line, and it really helps. I respect my husband; he respects me. If you give respect, you get respect. I think women are often the ones who set the tone of the house, with our attitudes and our moods, maybe because guys are a little less vocal, a little less emotional. We always try to set a respectful tone in my house so that things are peaceful.

A wonderful man wants you to feel his acceptance of you and will make efforts accordingly.

Corinne: I love my husband so much. I've always said to him, "You're a breath of fresh air," because he lets me be myself. In my earlier, abusive relationship, I was controlled and told how to do everything. But my husband is so different. I first met him in high school, and then remet him at our twenty-year high school reunion. I remember him being so special in school, because he made me laugh. I used to sit on the bench and talk with him, and all he did was make me laugh. I loved it. And I thought it was providential that he came back into my life twenty years later because I needed to laugh now. I'd lived a life of depression and oppression and despair in my relationship, and my husband came into my life to make me laugh and bring me joy. He is so wonderful. He let me be Corinne, who God made me to be. His acceptance of me has made it possible for me to grow in many ways; it's opened doors in my life that I never knew could exist for me. Now I minister to women; I teach aerobics. I've learned to speak in front of people, which I could never do before. My husband had been through a rocky relationship before, too, so when we came together, we knew, "This is what I want: for me to appreciate you and you to appreciate me." I'm so grateful to this man for helping me to learn life in this new way.

A wonderful man's acceptance of you expands your acceptance of yourself.

BEING ACCEPTED FOR who you are, just as you are, is a thing of beauty. It allows you to feel safe in the relationship, emotionally as well as physically. When you feel safe in a relationship, you relax. A certain level of stress disappears as you are bathed in the warm comfort of knowing that it's okay to be you. This is what Danielle experienced when her husband, learning of her past, responded with, "You're pure in my eyes." What an immense relief to her—so much so that she realized, "I think I could spend a lifetime with this man!"

A wonderful man makes you feel safe. Lots of men can say, "Oh, you're safe with me. I love you," but a wonderful man fulfills that promise by following through with actions. Danielle's husband could easily have said, when people looked askance at his car stuck in the mud, "Yeah, my wife, what can I tell you. Women drivers!" But he chose not to, and he preserved her emotional safety. When Corinne was upset and angry, her husband didn't respond as her abusive former husband had by yelling back at her or hitting her; he grabbed and hugged her, letting her know she was safe even in her anger. What a healing level of acceptance!

Certainly there were issues that needed to be talked about between Corinne and her husband. No relationship is all lovey-dovey, all the time, but a wonderful man will look for ways to discuss disagreements that preserve the emotional well-being of the couple. Her husband's acceptance of her even in the midst of her anger helped Corinne see that she didn't need to respond to her second husband as she had to her first husband. She was able to learn other ways to handle her anger so that she too could contribute to her marriage's emotional well-being.

Respect for each other is another way to express acceptance of each other. *Respect* means to regard highly, to have a sense of the worth of someone. When you respect someone, you don't interfere with his best interests; on the contrary, you strive to maintain those interests, among which is his safety and well-being. This is how Julia experiences the great difference between her prior relationship with an abusive husband and her current relationship with her wonderful man. They respect one another, and part of that respect is discussing issues without yelling or raising their voices. Another man may not care if he yells at you—"She deserved it! So what! I didn't hurt her"—as if physical blows were the only ones that hurt. Those who have been yelled at systematically know how verbal abuse damages your self-esteem, your self-worth—the very essence of your being. Accepting people as they are doesn't mean being on the receiving end of abuse. A wonderful man will neither dish it out nor accept it.

Recent research has stated unequivocally that emotional safety—being able to speak openly to one's partner about important issues in an atmosphere of emotional connection and support—is one of the fundamental attributes of a sound and healthy marriage. It is as important to a good relationship as personal safety—the freedom from fear of emotional or physical harm.

From that feeling of safety and security in the relationship, many good things are possible. You feel more confident about stepping forth into the world, about taking on greater challenges, reaching to be all that you are capable of. Corinne, for example, is eloquent in her expression of the many doors that her husband's acceptance of her has opened for her. She revels in being who she is and is eager to grow. She is deeply grateful to her husband for her "whole new life" and lets him know it in no uncertain terms. As we will see in later chapters, the feeling of emotional safety, coupled with a wonderful man's strong belief in you, is the foundation for the personal blossoming of so many of the Ladies' experiences.

There are men who do not accept us—men who, like Melody's beau, want you to wear makeup all the time or expect you to dress a certain way whether you want to or not. Men who, as Corinne's ex did, attempt to control you, telling you what you can and can't do regardless of how you feel about it. Men who, unlike Danielle's husband, are only too eager to tell you how stupid you are, how poorly you did this or that, or how dumb it was to do something that way.

They do not qualify as wonderful men.

How do you know the mark of a man who doesn't accept you as you are versus that of one who does? Here's how these men would respond differently to similar circumstances:

A man who does not accept you will say things like:	A man who accepts you will say:
"You look awful. What's the matter with you?"	"You don't look well. Are you feeling okay?"
"Can't you do anything right?"	"Are you having trouble with that? Would you like some help?"
"You're always forgetting things. It's really annoying."	"You've got a lot on your mind. It's easy to forget things."
"I can't believe you did that! How stupid." Or worse: "You're stupid."	"We all have our moments. Now what can I do to help?"

(Continued)

A man who does not accept you will say things like:	A man who accepts you will say:
"What, I gotta do everything around here? Princess can't lift a finger?"	"Looks like you're having a hard time with that. Can I lend a hand?"
"You're too sensitive! I can't say anything without you getting upset."	"I upset you. I'm sorry, I didn't mean to. Let me see if I can say that differently."

A man who does not accept you as you are will not want to hear your problems, your concerns, your issues. He will blame you for your weaknesses and failures. He will not show compassion for the flawed yet valiant human that you are, that we all are. He will not give himself graciously or willingly to help you with whatever your problems may be.

A man who accepts you as you are makes it safe for you to reveal your problems, your concerns, your issues. He understands that we all have vulnerabilities and seeks to support you through your challenges and difficulties. He helps you out, with ease and willingness, in whatever way he can.

More often than not, however, it's not our men who don't accept us—it's us. We don't accept ourselves as we are, which makes it very difficult for our men to do so. Do you remember in the fairy tale *Cinderella* how the prince asked all the women in the kingdom to try on the glass slipper so he could find his princess? The two ugly stepsisters wanted so much to win the handsome prince that they cut off pieces of their toes to squeeze their feet into the glass slipper. Many of us act like the stepsisters: we don't believe that a wonderful man will love us in our natural state, so we cut off pieces of ourselves.

Brainwashed as we've been by too many sex-laden commercials and reality makeover shows, we try to make ourselves fit some idea we have of the kind of woman a wonderful man would like. We fear rejection, so we don't present ourselves as we truly are—and we get rejected anyway. Or we find ourselves in relationships where we're not truly accepted, relationships in which we feel we have to cut off pieces of ourselves, our souls, in order to fit, as Melody did when she acceded to her meticulous boyfriend's demands that she dress and groom herself a certain way. We think, "Well, if I talk a certain way, or behave a certain way, or dress a certain way, he'll like me better. He'll love me," when in fact the opposite is true. A wonderful man will cherish you for the unique being you are. He will embrace the whole of you, not just certain parts, as if you were a side of beef, rib-eye versus tenderloin.

The more pieces of yourself you cut off, the less real the relationship is. One of the most marvelous aspects of being in a relationship with a wonderful man is that he will want you to be real. That is one of the few things he will expect of you: to be your real self, warts and all. Accepting yourself will make it possible for you to accept your mate as his real self. You must be secure enough with who you are to be okay with revealing that real self. You don't have to do it all at once and scare yourself half to death, but you do have to get there.

When you allow your man to see the whole of you, he can help you grow in whatever way pleases you. He can help you become more of who you really are, who, as Corinne says so eloquently "God made me to be."

When it comes to acceptance, what's good for the goose is good for the gander. Accepting your man as he is allows him to be. Nothing is more fulfilling than being loved just as you are. It is profoundly gratifying to a man to look into his woman's eyes and see that she truly accepts him. Make it safe for your man to disclose his real self. Give him the time and the space to do so.

Women are generally great talkers. We express ourselves freely to almost anybody, anytime, on just about any subject. We'll start a deep conversation while having our nails done, or during a commercial in response to the TV show we're watching. Men are quite different. For starters, men usually prefer to attend to one thing at a time. If they're watching TV, they're watching TV (don't be fooled by the channel surfing; they're still watching TV). If they're cooking, they're cooking. If they're changing a tire, they're changing a tire. Few men are comfortable doing any of the above *and* having a conversation about something else.

We know about the differences between us and our men not just from experience and anecdotes; biological research confirms these differences. Recent research has shown that male and female brains are composed of different amounts of gray and white matter. Our brains contain about 15 to 20 percent more gray matter than men's, which gives us more processing power. This gives us the multitasking abilities so often envied by our male friends and spouses. The white matter in our brains is found primarily in that area that links the brain's two hemispheres, which makes it easier for our brains to respond to verbal tasks—one of the reasons that we're usually better at talking than our partners are. Men have more white matter in their brains overall than we do, giving them that uncanny ability to parallel park in two swift, accurate maneuvers, as opposed to our three or more stabs at it. They can glance at the trunk of the car and say, "Oh, sure, that'll fit," while we say, "No way"—and then, yes, indeed, it does fit. The white matter is also what allows men to focus all their attention on one task, even if that does drive us nuts when we want his attention on several things at once.

Respect your man's biology! If you want to talk with your mate about a matter of consequence, make sure nothing else is going on so he doesn't feel torn between two (or more) points of attention. You are making the space safe for him.

It takes time for most men to divulge their innermost thoughts and feelings. Allow him that time. Sure, men will gab about superficial things—like weather, sports, and the stock market—quite readily, but when it comes to expressing their deeper feelings, their truths, forget it. A man must feel safe before he does that. He must feel that what he has to say won't be instantly judged—something we are all too eager to do—because that judgment almost always implies some sort of rejection.

When your man gives you his opinion on something, answers a question you've asked, or presents his idea about something, don't comment on it at first. Just listen. Give him a chance to elaborate on his thought without prompting. If a few minutes go by and he doesn't elaborate, say something innocuous like, "That's interesting. Tell me more." Then, once again, be quiet. Be attentive. Wait. Many men don't have thoughts ready to pop out on cue; they have to dig deep, rummage around in their minds. This means that their next thought will be considered, genuine. People who don't talk a lot tend to choose their words carefully. Give your man the time to come up with whatever it is he has to say.

You can make your man feel even safer by choosing not to counter his opinion or thought with one of your own at this point. Just thank him with, "That's cool, honey, thank you." That way your man learns that he can express himself without needing to enter a dialogue that he might not be up for at the moment or to defend his opinion. That's one of the reasons men get silent around us. We are forever demanding that they defend, explain, or rationalize their opinion, and hardly ever grant them the peace of mind of simply stating what they think or feel.

Later you can always pick the subject up again, and say, "You know, I've been thinking about what you said," and share your thoughts on the subject without turning the conversation into a debate.

Acceptance is not to be confused with approval. Approval is when someone is pleased with something you've said or done. Approval is great—it feels good—but it's not acceptance. Approval requires that you do or say something the other person likes; acceptance does not. Certainly, in a good relationship there will be lots of approval; otherwise you wouldn't be together. The problem is when you think your man will become wonderful if you do things he approves of. This is a trap that abused women often find themselves in. They think, "If only I don't ever look at another man, he won't get mad at me." "If I get dinner on the table on time, he won't be angry at me." "If I give him sex whenever he wants it, he won't get mad at me." Eventually you will find that you can never do enough to please an abusive individual.

A wonderful man will not necessarily approve of everything you say or do, and that's not the point. A wonderful man cares about you as you are, values you as you are, seeks to know and understand you as you are, and wants to help you find ways to be more and more yourself. If something you do or say upsets him, distresses him, or confuses him, he won't reject you for it. Instead, he'll sit down and talk it through with you. Lani's husband, for example, is concerned about her weight gain—not because it makes her less desirable in his eyes, and it certainly doesn't make him love her less, but because excess weight can have health consequences. He didn't turn off from her or constantly nag her about her weight, as another man might; rather, he discussed his concerns with her and accepted how she wanted to deal with them.

As wonderful as your man may be, there will be times that he does something you don't like, that you don't "approve" of. Rather than jump to the easy conclusion that "all men are pigs," or other such judgment, seek to understand why he would behave in that manner. Don't accuse him. Ask him what led to his doing something that troubles you. Say, "Honey, I'm confused, I thought we were budgeting for a new fridge," when he buys new golf clubs. This is far more likely to lead to a mutually fruitful discussion than, "What the heck were you thinking? That money was supposed to buy a new fridge!"

When you seek understanding, you are basically saying, "I know you're a good person. I know you want the best for us both in this relationship." This is a safe place of acceptance from which a conversation can proceed. Under these conditions, a good man can sit down with you and work it through, revealing his wonderfulness to you once again.

Week #3 of Your 35 Days to a Wonderful Man: Days 11–15

This week you'll:

- Identify and make peace with those parts of yourself you don't fully accept.
- Identify and make peace with those parts of your man you don't fully accept.
- Stop confusing acceptance with approval.
- Quit making it dangerous for your man to reveal his true self.
- Give your man the time and space to disclose his inner thoughts and feelings.

Day 11: Today I'll identify and make peace with the parts of myself I don't fully accept.

There are precious few of us who accept ourselves as we are, bumps and bunions included. But the less you accept yourself, the less you will reveal to your man, and the less he can accept and adore you for who you are. It's time to be courageous, to take a good look at yourself from all angles: physical, mental, emotional, and spiritual. Determine what you accept of your whole self, and ask yourself what pieces you cut off. It's not about liking every aspect of yourself: you may not like your weight or your tendency to go on shopping sprees when you're down, or that you get depressed for no apparent reason. It's about being real: accepting yourself as you are, like it or not. You can always choose to work on the parts you don't like, but you can't work on something you won't accept as a part of you. As you identify those cut-off parts of yourself, make peace with them. You do get depressed for no apparent reason. It's okay; you're human. You have trouble keeping your weight stable. It's okay; you're human! As you accept more and more of who you really are, you make it possible for a wonderful man to cherish and honor the whole of you.

Day 12: Today I'll identify and make peace with the parts of my man I don't fully accept.

No one is perfect—not even a wonderful man. You don't get to pick and choose parts of men—this guy's body, that other guy's morals, and this third one's brain. People are a package deal. When you fault your man for his lack of style, his loud laugh, his love of order, or whatever it is that you don't find acceptable, you reject him—all that is part of the package called "your man"—a package that has in it lots of parts you do accept: his kindness, his big heart, his way of keeping everything on track—whatever else it is. Just as it was necessary for you to identify and make peace with the parts of yourself you don't accept, so must you do the same with your man. This does NOT mean to accept abuse of any ilk (see the appendix). It does mean that if you don't like his sense of style, you can have fun helping him develop a new one rather than roll your eyes when he turns up in "that" shirt. If his laugh is loud, well, heck, he's enjoying himself. What could be better than that? As you accept more and more of who your man really is, you make it possible for him to relax, be his real self, and love you the more for it.

Day 13: Today I'll stop confusing acceptance with approval.

We all want approval from those we love. When you were a little girl, you wanted mommy or daddy to approve wholeheartedly of whatever you did, and you'd get their attention by yelling, "Look at me!!" Nothing has changed. We still want our loved ones to approve of everything we do. Acceptance, however, is not the same as approval. You can accept yourself fully, and not approve of some of the things you do or are. You can accept your occasional selfishness without approving of it. You can accept your yo-yo dieting without approving of it. You're not a bad or worthless person because of it.

Apply this concept to your man. Once you've revealed your true self to him, allow him to accept you without necessarily approving of everything you do or say. Don't confuse the two. Similarly, practice accepting the whole of your man, while at the same time approving of some of his behaviors and not of others. This means that although you don't approve of his dropping his wet towels on the bathroom floor, you will talk to him about wet towels on the bathroom floor in a problem-solving conversation. They are not a reason to shut him out, decide he's fit to live only in a sty, or think that he doesn't love you.

Day 14: Today I'll quit making it dangerous for my man to reveal his real self.

Notice how often you object to anything your man says, especially when he's offering advice or his opinion. If he says, "I need to go to the hardware store Saturday," the first words out of your mouth are likely to be, "Why?" or, "You're going there again?" as opposed to, "Oh, what were you thinking of getting?" If he says "I don't feel good today," you might blurt out, "I'm not surprised, given all the pizza you ate and beer you drank," rather than a simple, "I'm sorry. What do you think's going on?" Demanding, by word or tone, that your man constantly defend his every word or action makes it dangerous for him to reveal how he really feels or thinks. He's bound to feel attacked nine times out of ten! Today, every time you feel the urge to quiz him or inform him of why he thinks or feels as he does, stop. Take a deep breath, and either say nothing or ask him, nonjudgmentally, "What's going on?" The less judgment you impose on your man, the more he can be his real self with you.

Day 15: Today I'll give my man the time and space to disclose his inner thoughts and feelings.

Most men need a safe space in which to reveal themselves and a safe time in which to do so. Don't start a deep, meaningful conversation when he's busy with other things. Create the space for him to focus on what you want to talk about. Suggest taking a walk together, or going for a drive to somewhere peaceful. Or sit together on your back porch, where you can be alone and at peace. You learned on Day 14 how to refrain from attacking your man for what he reveals to you. Now you'll take it one step further by giving him time to express himself. Don't rush to give your opinion or advice. Take a breath. Say, "Tell me more," rather than, "Why?" Allow a conversation to unfold over a period of hours or even days. Give your man the time and space to express himself, and you'll receive the joy of his true self rather than the nervous evasion of a cornered being.

Use the weekend to repeat whichever of the days were more challenging for you.

Keep track of your progress daily on your "How Did I Do Today?" chart. Enter check marks to keep track of how you did: one check for "Yes, I did," two checks for "Yes, I really did," or three for "I was brilliant on this one!" and either a minus or zero if you didn't do the item. You'll be able to see at a glance how you're doing.

Remember to keep practicing the past weeks' items as you go forward with this week's plan.

How Did I Do Today?

Days 11–15

Item	Day 11	Day 12	Day 13	Day 14	Day 15	SAT	SUN
Did I identify and make peace with the parts of myself I don't fully accept?							
Did I identify and make peace with the parts of my man I don't fully accept?							
Did I stop confusing acceptance with approval?							
Did I quit making it dangerous for my man to reveal his real self?							
Did I give my man the time and space to disclose his inner thoughts and feelings?							

Human beings, like plants, grow in the soil of acceptance, not in the atmosphere of rejection.

JOHN POWELL, *British composer*

CHAPTER 4

BELIEVING IN EACH OTHER

A WONDERFUL MAN believes in you.

A wonderful man supports your dreams and your desires. He's your biggest cheerleader, bar none. He encourages you to pursue whatever inspires and enthralls you, even when you're quaking in your boots. When you ask, "Can I do it? Can I really?" he says, "Yes, all the way. You go, girl!" A wonderful man believes in you when you don't. He sees your potential when you can't. He is your most ardent supporter.

A wonderful man wants you to be and do and have whatever it is you want to be and do and have. He doesn't just give your dreams lip service, saying, "That's nice, dear, you go right on ahead and do that." He's truly by your side, mentally, physically, and emotionally, every step of the way.

A wonderful man will willingly sacrifice his time, his effort, even his prize possessions to help you reach your goals. And he won't complain, hold it against you, or throw his sacrifice back at you in a moment of anger or upset. A wonderful man does what he does because he wants to, so there's no resentment or regret down the line.

May: I'm a stay-at-home mom—I have two young kids—but I didn't start out that way. Before we had kids, I was a clinical pharmacist. In fact, I knew nothing about being a housewife or a mom. They don't teach you how to do these things in school! But my husband has encouraged me to look into these different areas—to search, to develop areas that I'd never discovered in myself before. Like a couple of years back when we moved into a new home, we needed drapes for the living room. I had taken some sewing lessons in junior high, but that was it. We had these thirteen-foot-high windows, and I told my husband, "You know what? I'm gonna make drapes for them." I didn't even own a sewing machine, and my husband had never seen me sew anything, ever, but he did not bat an eye. He just told me, "Okay, we've got to find a sewing machine." I picked out a pretty good one, not the cheapest one, and then I went to the fabric store. Thankfully, I have a friend who's a seasoned seamstress, so she took me there and helped with measuring and buying the fabric. I bought eighty yards of fabric—and my husband wasn't shocked or anything, although I was. That's a lot of fabric! But he encouraged me. And he let me make a huge mess in our living room to make these big panels, and later when he knew that I was thinking about decorating the house, he bought me books to help me with that too.

A wonderful man supports your projects with actions as well as words.

Melody: I felt very supported by my husband to pursue my dreams, whatever I want to do. Sometimes I'd think, "Omi-gosh, I don't know if I want to be supported that much!" because he often has more confidence in me than I do. That's something I really appreciate. It challenges me, it sharpens me, it makes me grow, and it makes me think he's on my team. He wants me to be the best that I can be in all that I want to do. He never makes me feel like he's thinking, "Oh, you're a woman, you can't do this," or anything like that.

A wonderful man believes that anything you want is within your capabilities.

Lani: My husband was a big encouragement as I got my master's. I felt that I wanted to do something new when our kids were grown. I had been to college, but then I had the kids and became a stay-at-home mom. It was really tough for me to go back to school after all those years, but my husband was my cheerleader. He would cheer me on, saying, "You can do it!" and, "Continue, go ahead, go on," when I'd get discouraged. Even though it took a while for me to complete my degree, he was always there for me, cheering me on. When I completed it, I felt it wasn't just my accomplishment, because my husband helped me get there.

A wonderful man cheers you on all the way to your goal, no matter how distant the goal is or how long it takes to get there.

Linda: From the beginning of our relationship, my husband had a dream and a desire to go to a school in California. We were originally both at college in Texas, but he wanted to go to this school in California where there was a certain professor who was the top in his field—someone Jack really wanted to study under. He was inspired by the professor and wanted the benefit of this professor's particular training and teaching. He felt it was extremely important to his future. Well, I didn't want to rob him of that, even though I was attending Texas State and felt like I needed to stay there. At that time he was my boyfriend. So even though most women would tend to say, "No, stay here with me!" I said, "I think you should go for it," even though I knew that it would be a sacrifice for me because I would see him just once every six months. But I also knew that he would ultimately resent me for caging him in, and I didn't want that to happen. I feel like I empowered him, which in turn gave him the desire to encourage and empower me. We got engaged while I was still at Texas State and he was in California. Then he flew home, we got married, and we moved out to California. By then I was out of college and was fine with moving.

When you're with a wonderful man, believe in him as he believes in you.

Linda: I love dreaming with my husband about different things. Who knows if it'll ever happen? But it's really cool, taking steps to pursue our dreams, encouraging each other to try something new or take some sort of risk. I value his thoughts and his dreams every bit as much as he does mine. It's really neat, because as you encourage each other, you can see the other person develop, as I've seen Jack step out of his insecurities. I'm sure he's seen me do the same.

Believing in each other is rewarding to both of you.

Olivia: My husband is amazing because he is so supportive of me. I'm an actress, and I've started directing theater. And

I have a four-year-old, and I'm eight months pregnant. And I'm just crazy enough that I'm still out there doing theater. He always lets me do projects if I want to and helps make them possible. He will take care of our daughter so I can do my thing. I just directed a theatrical reading. I came home, and I had all these ideas about what I wanted to do with it, to play with sound and so on. I wasn't sure if I should go through with my ideas, or if I should just let it be a straight reading with the actors all sitting down. My husband said to me, "I don't think you should be conservative. I think you should just do it. If you go for it and you do it, at least you tried to do something, and if it doesn't work, who cares? At least you tried something." And I wasn't sure and told him I didn't know if I could pull it off. What if someone didn't like it? And he said, "You have this idea—you should just go for it." That really gave me the confidence to go to the theater the next day and say, "Okay, everybody, we're going to do it like this." Because my husband had instilled that confidence in me, the reading went very well, it was well received, and I was proud of what happened. That's because of him.

When a wonderful man believes in you, your confidence and belief in yourself increase.

MARY is forty-eight years old, Caucasian, married for twenty-five years to her fifty-four-year-old Hispanic husband, Ben, a truck driver. She's the head cashier at a local supermarket. For both, it's a first marriage. They have three children.

Mary: Our mom had Alzheimer's. I wasn't working at the time, but both my sisters were, so I helped take care of my mother. My father had taken care of my mother for the longest time, but my father had cancer, and eventually he couldn't care for her anymore. My dad had always been the go-to guy. He could fix anything, he could take care of everything, but he couldn't fix this. I ended up moving into my parents' home, along with my husband and our one son who was still living at home, to help my father take care of her. I would get up at 5:00 A.M. to take my son to school, and my dad would ask me to hurry back, because my mom would need me. That was a huge sacrifice for my husband. I would say to my husband, "I know this is hard," and he would say, "Well, you helped with my parents." My dad cried to my husband, saying, "I know what this is doing to your family. I know the sacrifice you are making by my taking your wife, my daughter, away from you. I want you to know how much this means to me."

My father was fiercely independent: he didn't want or need anything from anybody. He was a giver and he was happy being a giver, so being on the receiving end like this was really painful for him.

My husband and I have been married twenty-five years, and it's not perfect—we have our ups and downs—but I will be eternally grateful to him because I was able to be there for my mom and dad when I really wanted to be. A lot of men wouldn't have accepted this. It was a huge sacrifice. Our lives were turned upside down for almost a year, but my husband was right there through it all. He supported me and he helped and did whatever had to be done. I am eternally grateful to him for not making me feel guilty, not complaining about the burden I had put on the family, not then or anytime after that.

A wonderful man supports all your endeavors—not just the easy ones.

Lucy: When you come into a marriage, you have this pre-conceived idea of who your new husband is and who you are. I think that going through a relationship is like peeling away the layers of the onion. It's getting to that place where you get to know that person by being real, by trusting them and realizing that we can help each other be all that we can be. And it goes both ways. My husband really believes in me. He's invested a lot of effort and money in encouraging and supporting me as I pursued my career. It makes me nervous because he's invested so much, but he's saying, "You can do this. You're putting it out there, and you can do this." And because he believes in me so strongly, I'm doing way more than I ever thought possible. It blows me away that he can believe in me that much. And I ask myself, "Am I doing the same for him?" I hope I am, I try to, but I always think that I could do so much more.

To be as enthusiastic and encouraging of your wonderful man as he is of you is to cheerlead in the grandest and best sense.

Nancy: I started dating my husband when I was in high school. He reads me so well. We have three daughters, and when they were little, he knew when I needed a break. He'd say, "Honey, I'll pick up the dishes, run a bath for you, and put the kids to bed." I'd go into the bathroom, and there'd be candles, and he'd say, "Just enjoy yourself." Sometimes I'd be in the bath so long that he'd knock on the door and ask, "Are you okay?" He'd know when I needed to escape, when I needed time for myself.

For the past seventeen years or so, I've met with my girl-friends about three Mondays a month. We just do crafts or talk. We don't bash our men; we're there to encourage each other. We're supportive of each other, we've helped each other with our kids, and we've held each other together through rough times. He knows how important my friends are to me, and he's great with it. He knows that's my night.

Even now that our children are older, he knows when we need a break. He'll say, "Come on, let's go," and we'll just pick up and go somewhere for a night. We'll take a guidebook and start calling around after 6:00, because that's when hotel rates go down. He's always been that way, thoughtful of my needs, and so once the kids graduated from high school, I said, "Okay, honey, it's your turn to pick a vacation—anywhere you want to go, whatever you want to do," because until then, all our vacations, except for those occasional one-night getaways, were always for the kids, and he was always willing to do it, no complaints. I really appreciated that.

Well, my husband decided we were going to go kayak-ing. With whales. We would kayak from one uninhabited is-land to the next, looking for whales. And neither of us had ever kayaked before. It had to be the hardest thing I've ever done. We thought we'd have dual kayaks, meaning we'd both be in the same kayak, but when we got there, it was single kayaks. So there I am, in the middle of the ocean, kayaking away all on my own, following him. On top of it all, we slept in tents, and it rained and thundered and there was lightning. It was something! Once the kayaking trip was over, he said, "You've been such a good sport about all this, I know it wasn't your cup of tea, how about if we stay over at a bed and breakfast for a couple of days before we go home?" I said, "Oh, thank you!" I stayed in that big, comfy bed-and-breakfast bed almost the whole two days. That wasn't in our plan, but my husband knew he had to find a way to fill me back up. That's how he reads me: he knows just what I need right when I need it. He's my best friend.

Rooting for each other's dreams and desires isn't done at arm's length. It's hands on, all the way.

Mary: When my husband and I got married, we had a plan, a common goal. Once we had kids, we said we were going to do our best to send our kids to private school and for me to be able to stay home. That was the plan. And it worked for a while, but then stuff happened and things got financially tight. I couldn't see how we were going to be able to keep our two boys in private school. I remember saying to him, "You know, honey, we can put our younger son in a public school and allow the older one to go to private school and I can get a job." I was trying really hard to convince him, and he said, "That is out of the question. We had a goal in the beginning. If I have to get a second job, I will get a second job for you to be able to stay home and keep the kids in private school." And that's what he did.

My husband's a truck driver. He would drive all day, then he would come home, eat, and drive again part time at night. In the meantime, he always coached the kids' games. I remember times when he would work all night, get home about eight in the morning, and he'd coach a baseball game at eleven. He'd stay up, coach the game, and in order to spend time with the kids, he'd stay up until well into the night and then he'd fall asleep, only to get up early and start all over again. So that really blessed me, because it was really important to us for me to stay at home and be with the kids. To keep other expenses down, we drove our cars until the doors fell off. Literally. We shopped at thrift stores, did whatever we had to do, and my husband never ever said, "I'd like to have this," or, "It's because of these kids I can't have my dream car," or whatever. I really appreciated that he did all that.

The kids are older now and out of school, plus we received a small inheritance, so we have a little money again. It's cute: my husband saw a Corvette and he said, "Hmmm," and I said, "Mmm, maybe not the Corvette, but we could start with a nice Toyota Camry," and he hugged me really hard and said, "Okay."

A wonderful man works unstintingly to fulfill the goals you set together.

GRACE is forty years old to her husband, Mitch's, forty-two. They are both Caucasian, and have been married for eighteen years. They have six children, ranging in age from four to sixteen. She's a homemaker; he's a corporate vice president. This is a first marriage for both.

Grace: I have six children. I'm a stay-at-home mom. Well, with that many kids, you sort of have to be. I appreciate my husband's commuting in bumper-to-bumper traffic every day to duke it out in the corporate world and then bringing home that paycheck for us to spend. When he gets home,

the ice cream he paid for is gone, his dinner might be macaroni and cheese three nights in a row, and his suits are off
the rack. For about three years, he took the bus to work because we had only one car. He let me have the car and took
the bus, and he didn't complain. Ever. Meanwhile his friends
who are single get a new car every two years, have fancy
lifestyles, and go out all the time. He gives everything to us
and doesn't complain. I appreciate that so much.

*A wonderful man doesn't complain about what it takes to make your
life together work the way you want it to.*

Melia: Jorge has never ceased to amaze me or our kids (all
three girls) with his willingness to sacrifice for me and the
family. When I gave birth to our first daughter, I had to continue to work and did so following the six-week maternity
leave. Financially, we just wouldn't have been able to make
it without my paycheck. I not only worked as a secretary
but volunteered as church secretary. Because I worked, I
was able to use company computers to perform my secretarial duties for the church.

Well, after I had my second daughter, I wasn't physically
able to go back to work right away. I ended up having to
stay home for one year. As you can imagine, this put us even
at a greater disadvantage financially, and we wound up having my husband's dream car, a 528i BMW, repossessed. Not
once did my husband complain. Though I felt like gum un-
derneath his shoe and though he wasn't thrilled, he didn't
make me feel worthless, and he didn't shame me. And to
this day, he has never brought it up. Jorge wound up taking
the bus to and from work or, when possible, he'd carpool

with a coworker. More often than not, Jorge took the bus because he didn't want me to be without a car in case there was an emergency with the kids.

Well, since I was no longer working, I didn't have access to a computer or typewriter, so I was worried I would need to give up volunteering my secretarial services for our church. So what does the love of my life do? Unbeknown to me, Jorge sold his most prized possession—one of two guitars. Jorge took me to the store and told me to go look at typewriters. I told him that we couldn't afford it. Jorge then said, "Just humor me. Go look, so when we get money, we can come back and purchase it." Well, I did. I chose a Brother typewriter that also had memory capacity. I don't remember how much it cost because that was seventeen years ago. Jorge then bought the typewriter and informed me that he had sold his favorite guitar. I cried tears of appreciation and joy that he would love and care so much for me. I still have the typewriter to this day. No boyfriend could rival that. And that's the truth! What is even more glorious to me about this act of love is that my favorite story of all time is "Gift of the Magi" by O. Henry. The couple was experiencing financial woes. Just like the husband in the story who sold his grandfather's watch to buy his wife combs for her hair, Jorge sold his most prized possession so I could continue providing secretarial services for our church. Doesn't that just warm your heart? This is an eternal memory.

A wonderful man cares more about making your dreams come true than he does about whatever sacrifices he has to make.

A WONDERFUL MAN supports your dreams and desires not because he has to, but because he wants to. And the more you appreciate his support, the more likely he is to want to keep on giving it to you. It's just plain old common sense, and yet so often, we fail to appreciate that support. We find fault with how our mate supports us, or how much, or how little, or when he does so, instead of simply appreciating what is being offered when it is being offered. We ignore or don't even see many of the ways in which our mates are being supportive, and so we don't appreciate, we don't give thanks, we aren't grateful.

And if anything you focus on grows, the opposite is just as true: whatever you don't focus on dies. Your mate's encouragement, his cheerleading, his sacrifices, if left unnoticed and unappreciated, will dwindle, diminish, and eventually cease entirely.

How easy it would have been for May to be unaware of the support her husband offered by letting her make her "huge mess" in the living room. She could have just thought, "Well, heck, it's my living room too!" and not even noticed the support implicit in her husband's putting up with the "mess." When he bought her books on decorating, May wisely saw her husband's efforts as encouraging her efforts, whereas another woman might have thought, "So he thinks I can't do it on my own. He thinks I'm too stupid to figure it out," and felt disrespected rather than supported.

When Nancy's husband says, "Come on, let's go," because he feels the two of them need a break, Nancy says, "Great!" and off they go, guidebook in hand. Nancy does not say, as many women might, "What do you mean, you haven't made a reservation? What if we don't find a nice place? Where are we going to have dinner?" She doesn't devalue his support by complaining about having to find a lower hotel rate. She doesn't say to herself, "He can't even earn enough to afford a normal room rate. What a loser I married." Instead, she appreciates his effort for what it is: giving her a break, a rest—in a word, support.

Melia speaks lovingly and appreciatively of her husband's willingness to let his dream car, a 528i BMW, be repossessed so that she could recuperate at home. How different her attitude is from that of a woman who might instead blame her husband for not getting a better job, not earning more income, which would allow him to maintain their previous lifestyle! So too does Grace praise her husband's willingness to take the bus to work so that she could have the use of their one car.

Too often we simply rag on our man to make more money, or call him a loser for not doing better. We compare him to other men in a way that makes him come out on the bottom. This isn't surprising, as we are genetically and hormonally programmed for our biological imperative: making babies. It doesn't matter whether you have children or not, whether you want them ardently or cringe at the thought. You are, as a woman, built for bearing children. As such, we seek out mates who will provide for those children, and will protect and defend them, as well as ourselves. This is just as true if you are a dyed-in-the-wool homemaker with six children or if you have a professional career and earn twice what your man makes and think of children as a "maybe" or "never." Your biology doesn't know the difference. You are more likely than not to be attracted to a strong, healthy male who is hardworking and goal-oriented, with an optimistic, prosperous vision of his future. Let's face it: Have you ever said or heard a girlfriend say, "Oh, I don't want a strong, healthy man who has ambition and the energy and determination to reach his goals. No, I want a weak, sickly guy with no ambition, who's lazy, pessimistic and wouldn't know how to set a goal"? Never going to happen!

So when a man gives up his BMW or takes the bus to work, even if it's a sacrifice lovingly made to support his wife, many women are programmed to fear that "it's all downhill from here." They worry, even if only on a subconscious level, that their man can't provide—

that it starts with giving up the BMW and ends with giving up the home. These fears are then communicated to their partner as blame: "How come you can't earn more?" "Well if you worked harder, like so-and-so's husband, maybe we could afford two cars and I wouldn't have to be embarrassed when someone sees you riding the bus." If the woman is insecure about her own ability to provide for herself and her family, these fears may be aggravated further, causing her to reject her partner's self-sacrifice even more caustically: "You're such a loser! That's the best you can do—ride the bus?!" A man can hardly reveal his wonderfulness when he's emotionally on the ground with your foot on his neck.

If you find yourself thinking less of your man when he makes a sacrifice to support you, whatever that sacrifice may be, stop and ask yourself, "What am I afraid of here?" Is it that you don't trust his capacity to hold up his end of the marital agreement, whether he's the sole provider for the whole family or an occasional contributor? Is it that you're afraid his way of coping with difficulties is to give things up rather than seek to grow and expand? Is it that you're afraid that eventually you will have to take charge of far more than you feel capable of? Whatever you fear, be honest with yourself. You can't deal with a fear until you face it. Then sit down and talk with your man. Let him know, first of all, how grateful you are for his sacrifice. Then discuss the fears that you'd like to talk about with him. A wonderful man will respect you for bringing up your fears and will be willing to talk them through in a way that brings you closer.

At other times we take completely for granted the support our mates offer us. It's as if they were invisible, and the efforts they make to help us don't exist. That is painful for our mates. When Olivia's husband looks after their daughter so she can pursue her theatrical career, she is grateful. She doesn't think, "Well, he should! He's her father." She thinks, "Wow, he's being so supportive of me." When Mary's husband helped out with her mom's Alzheimer's, Mary was not only grateful to her mate for standing by her and doing whatever needed to be done, but also for his not making her feel guilty about the imposition on him and their family. Many women may not even have thought about being appreciative of the guilt-free support. They would simply have thought, "Well, it's nice that he helped, but he had to, didn't he," and failed to see the extra support their husbands' emotional restraint gave them.

How many of us think to thank our mates for simply doing their jobs or, as Grace puts it, "duking it out in the corporate world, day after day"? For putting up with the traffic, the politics of the workplace, the jockeying for position, the demands of the job itself, whether he's a cement pumper or a heart surgeon. Just because you may also be in the workforce doesn't mean that you can't appreciate your mate's support and the benefits his work brings you and your family.

Appreciate your mate's supportiveness—all that he does to demonstrate his ardent belief in you. If you never take his support for granted, you will sustain your mate's desire to be your most zealous fan. Heck, he'll twirl a baton and invest in pom-poms if it will help you get where you want to be going. Just be sure to let him know just how much you value his many contributions to your success and joy.

Sometimes what stands in the way of your appreciation of your mate's efforts to support you is your lack of belief in yourself. Melody touched on that when she said that her husband often has more confidence in her ability to do something than she does. If you don't believe in yourself, your mate's cheerleading can feel like too much pressure—an obligation you must live up to rather than an uplifting joy.

Believing in yourself has everything to do with knowing your qualities. Your qualities are your strengths. They are the assets you have available to you to help you achieve your goals and cope successfully with life's challenges. If you don't know your strengths, how can you feel confident that you even have a chance of realizing your dreams, your desires? If you aren't confident and don't believe in yourself, you will be hard-pressed to appreciate your man's support—you'll be too conflicted by your own lack of belief. Women often hesitate to acknowledge their qualities, even to themselves, yet by not acknowledging your qualities, you undermine your ability to succeed.

Discovering and acknowledging your qualities isn't difficult; it just takes a little introspection. We all have qualities, so don't worry; you won't come up short.

Your qualities exist on three levels: mental, emotional/spiritual, and physical. Take a good look at each and figure out your unique qualities. Physically, for example, ask yourself, "What do I like about my physical being? What do I consider my strong points?" Think about what people have commented on over the years. Do people tell you what a winsome smile you have, or how you always seem to be in great shape? Then ask yourself, "What have I always prided myself on mentally? What have people noticed about my mind?" There is more to mental qualities than IQ; mental qualities are about how you think. For example, are you great at seeing the trees (specifics) or better at seeing the forest (big picture)? Are you good at coming up with concepts or better at structuring practical matters? And so on. Repeat this process with the emotional/spiritual level. What do you like about yourself in this arena? What aspects of your character have people noticed over the years? Your kindness? Your outspokenness? Your perseverance? Your caring nature?

Make yourself aware of how your qualities play out in your daily life. Once you understand how they serve you now, you can develop them further or develop new ones, and your self-confidence, your belief in yourself, will grow accordingly.

Supporting your man is just as important as appreciating the support he gives you. Yours can't be the only dream that matters. Treasure his aspirations, and applaud his strivings. Give everything you can to further his desires. Let your man know, in words and deeds, that you believe in him, that you are every bit as convinced of his ability to have and be all that he can, just as he is of yours.

As Linda pointed out, when her boyfriend wanted to leave Texas and study in California, most women might have objected and said, "No, stay with me!" Yet Linda was willing to set aside whatever unhappiness his absence would cause her because she believed in him and wanted him to fulfill his dreams. Her supportiveness empowered her mate and nourished his ability to be a wonderful man. In much the same way, Nancy set aside her idea of a great vacation to support her husband's kayaking dream—something she never would have chosen to do.

Just as acknowledging your qualities is important to your self-confidence, knowing your mate's qualities makes it possible for you to genuinely say, "I believe in you." Give some thought to your mate's physical, mental, and emotional qualities. So much of the time we know all about our mate's weaknesses but very little about his strengths. Familiarize yourself with his strengths and how they play out in the real world so you can remind him of those strengths when it's your turn to cheerlead and twirl that baton.

A wonderful man believes in you. Believe just as much in him, and the possibilities for your success and joy are infinite.

Week #4 of Your 35 Days to a Wonderful Man: Days 16–20

This week you'll:

Discover the many ways in which your man supports and encourages you.

Stop finding fault with how he cheers you on.

Demonstrate your appreciation of his support and encouragement.

Define and appreciate your man's qualities.

Encourage and support your man's dreams and desires.

Day 16: Today I'll discover the many ways in which my man supports and encourages me.

Today you'll go beyond the obvious—the times your man literally says, "I'm happy to support you in this," to discover the many other ways in which he supports and encourages you. There's the newspaper article he brings to your attention that has to do with a new project you've embarked on. There's his quiet acceptance of macaroni and cheese for five days in a row while you're on a sewing binge. There's his giving up golf day to help you clean out your side of the garage, or his piping up with, "You know, I think I know someone who can help you with that," when you've come up against a roadblock on your personal path. These are all ways your man supports and encourages your dreams and desires, sometimes at the expense of his. Today you'll make a list of all these not-so-obvious instances of support over the past couple of months. Just for the fun of it, make a list of the obvious ones too.

Day 17: Today I'll stop finding fault with how he cheers me on.

We all have our ideas of how things should be done. That's normal. When your mate cheers you on, maybe by maxing out his credit card to get that gizmo for you, we're all too prone to say, "Oh, you shouldn't have. It's much too expensive, and I could have fixed the old gizmo." Or when he brings the newspaper article to your attention, you might say, "That's old news; I saw that last week," or a condescending, "That's nice, dear." Stop doing that! Slapping the hand that gives you a gift is guaranteed to put an end to the giving. Your man wants and needs to support your efforts, and he needs the freedom to support you in ways that make sense to him. Today you will stop finding fault with those ways. Start by jotting down the ways you've criticized your man's efforts to support or encourage you in the past couple of months. Be honest with yourself. Sometimes your tone or manner is the criticism. We say a great deal without words. Your man's support and encouragement of what matters to you is a big part of what's wonderful in him. If you discourage him by finding fault, that wonderfulness will quickly be squelched.

Day 18: Today I'll demonstrate my appreciation of his support and encouragement.

You've made a good start by ceasing to find fault with your man's support and encouragement. Now let's take it a step further. Today you'll actively demonstrate your sincere appreciation of his support and encouragement. The key word here is *sincere*. If you wish he hadn't spent so much money on the gizmo, then that's not where you focus your appreciation because you'd be less than honest. You can appreciate his concern for the success of your project and his thoughtfulness in getting you the gizmo. You can appreciate the time and energy he put into researching getting just the right gizmo for you.

There's lots to be grateful for without resorting to half-truths or outright lies. Then there are all the nonverbal ways in which you can demonstrate your appreciation. Your smile and hug, when you cuddle closer on the couch—these are demonstrations of appreciation. Telling others in front of him how grateful you are for his encouragement is another. Today you'll offer as many sincere demonstrations of your appreciation of your man's encouragement and support as you can think of. If you can think of only one way, great! Start there. Tomorrow you can think of more.

Day 19: Today I'll define and appreciate my man's qualities.

Your man will continue to be your best cheerleader as you both appreciate his efforts on your behalf and become his most enthusiastic supporter. The better you know your man, the easier it is to genuinely and effectively support him. Today you'll get to know your man better by defining and appreciating his qualities. Start by making a list of his qualities: honesty, courage, creative vision, perseverance, positive attitude. Then pick one, and let him know how terrific that quality is, how it contributes to his success or happiness. Praising his perseverance, for example, you might say, "I was thinking, hon, how lucky they are to have you at work—you always see things through, even when the going gets rough." Or in appreciating his positive attitude, you might say, "When you helped your Little Leaguers see the games they lost as an opportunity to make some much-needed changes instead of as a losing streak, your positive outlook sure made a difference to those kids." Today you will make the effort to identify and praise your man's qualities, one quality at a time if that's what it takes.

Day 20: Today I'll encourage and support my man's dreams and desires.

Today you will encourage and support your man's dreams and desires, for they are no less important than yours. You may find that you don't really know what those dreams and desires are anymore, for once past the honeymoon phase, we often get caught up in daily living and don't spend lovely romantic nights chatting about our dreams into the wee hours. We're more likely to be trying to catch up on sleep. Here's your opportunity to go back to your sweet beginnings and ask your man what his current dreams and desires are. Today, make a concerted effort to encourage and support those dreams and desires. Don't judge them as less important than yours, frivolous, or otherwise unworthy. Don't analyze or criticize his dreams; simply accept them as his, and cheer him on enthusiastically. If some of his dreams seem risky or foolish, you can have conversations with him about your concerns later and help him figure out appropriate solutions or less scary alternatives. For now, focus on wholeheartedly supporting those dreams.

Use the weekend to repeat whichever of the days were more challenging for you.

Keep track of your progress daily on your "How Did I Do Today?" chart. Enter check marks to keep track of how you did: one check for "Yes, I did," two checks for "Yes, I really did," or three for "I was brilliant on this one!" and either a minus or zero if you didn't do the item. You'll be able to see at a glance how you're doing.

Remember to keep practicing the past weeks' items as you go forward with this week's plan.

How Did I Do Today?

Days 16–20

Item	Day 16	Day 17	Day 18	Day 19	Day 20	SAT	SUN
Did I discover the many ways in which my man supports and encourages me?							
Did I stop finding fault with how he cheers me on?							
Did I demonstrate my appreciation of his support and encouragement?							
Did I define and appreciate my man's qualities?							
Did I encourage and support my man's dreams and desires?							

Treat people as if they were what they ought to be and you help them to become what they are capable of being.

JOHANN WOLFGANG VON GOETHE

CHAPTER 5

TRUE FORGIVENESS

A WONDERFUL MAN is one who forgives.

A wonderful man doesn't hold things against you. He readily forgives you and others. He is quick to apologize if you are wounded, even when he doesn't know what part—if any—he may have played in your hurt.

A wonderful man would much rather solve problems than create them. He's more interested in loving than in being right, in moving forward toward mutual satisfaction and fulfillment than in staying stuck in blame or anger, in understanding your point of view than in indulging his self-righteousness.

Danielle: When I was growing up, I would give the silent treatment if I didn't like something. I was the youngest and the only girl, so it worked like a charm. With Charlie, my husband, I tried to do the same thing. If he did something I didn't like, I'd just give him the silent treatment. But he would ask, "Did I do something wrong?" I'd say, "No." "Have

I offended you?" "No." I wanted to make him work for it. But he wouldn't buy in to it. He'd just wait, ask me again, and when I wouldn't answer, he'd finally say, "When you're finished, I'll be in the other room."

Early on, even when we were dating, Charlie would say straight out, "This bothered me," or, "You've offended me." I was totally blown out of the water. I'd say, "What?!" But because he was willing to come to me and tell me what had bothered or offended him, I felt free to do the same. And the wonderful part is that he forgives, as do I. So it does help, being willing to say what's troubling you and working it out together, with forgiveness. It helps you to grow.

Knowing your wonderful man is forgiving makes it easier to work things out together.

LATAESHA, thirty-two years old, is African American. She works as a teacher. Her husband, Geoff, thirty-three years old, is Puerto Rican and is a construction foreman. They've been married five years. It's a first marriage for both, no kids.

Lataesha: Early on I had a lot of anger and bitterness in my heart from my life before I got married. My husband is just this teddy bear with so much love, but it was still very difficult for me in the beginning to receive the love that he was willing to give to me. Also, my parents are divorced, so most of what I learned about marriage was from seeing my parents argue. I never really saw any good, healthy examples of a loving marriage around me up until the time I got married. So when I got married, it was a very difficult thing for me to really let down my guard and let him fully love and care for me. He was always willing to forgive and say, "I love you," and all these things. I, on the other hand, would say, "Huh! You make me mad," and go silent. That was the only coping mechanism that I knew. Eventually I realized that the silent treatment is so wrong and that I had to stop doing that.

My husband was always willing to be the first one to apologize, to come to me and say, "You know, I love you and I care about you. We're gonna get through this. Let's be friends." This is what helped me be receptive to that change. I was very appreciative that he was so willing to love, and not fall for my silent routine. I had dealt with so much that I was always afraid of being rejected, so my knee-jerk reaction to any upset was to reject first. He was free from that. He didn't deal with that, and he took the risk of loving even though he might not at that moment receive love in return. He really helped me to see that he is trustworthy; he is trustworthy of my heart. As the process has continued, I'm just very appreciative that he helped me understand the safety of loving and being loved, that things can happen but you can talk it out and forgive and keep loving. He initiated that, and our relationship, our love, is strong because of that.

A wonderful man's forgiveness makes it safe for you to fully love and be loved.

Anne: My dad was a great dad, but he was an only child and a pouter. My parents were married for sixty-four years, but I don't think I ever heard my dad say, "I'm sorry." When I got married to Jesse, it was really strange for me to hear Jesse say, "You know, I don't think I did anything wrong, but I'm sorry," and even though I'd know I was the one who did something wrong, I was determined not to apologize first. He'd always say, "I'm sorry," first. And it would break the ice. It was almost as if there was only one thing I could do: "Well, stupid, now I have to say I'm sorry." Jesse literally said, "It's a choice you make, to forgive." He actually even wrote a song called "Choose to Forgive." And he always wanted to make that choice, definitely before we went to bed at night and preferably before we left the room. He didn't want our love to be divided. He wanted us to be able to still be one in our hearts, to be in agreement about whatever it was.

I just always think that's an amazing thing about him. He'll make the choice to apologize, even when he knows he isn't wrong, because many times I was wrong. He's made that choice so many times in front of our children. He's set that example for them. There's a wonderful freedom that is set loose in the relationship when you can forgive and be forgiven.

A wonderful man knows that forgiveness is a choice and consciously makes that choice.

Linda: My husband has a great sense of humor. That's just been wonderful, because we never take each other too seriously on the small things. Like every Tuesday is trash day. Sometimes he forgets to take the trash out. Some people would badger him and say, "Well, you should have taken the trash out," or whatever. Instead, if he's forgotten to take the trash out, I'll say, "Ah, there's nothing like the smell of rotten garbage in the garage," and he says, "Yeah, I forgot." I say, "Oh, well, more for the garbage man next time"—you know, make light of it, make it something funny. We never take it too seriously. Life's just too short to squabble about the small things.

Forgiving the little things protects the closeness between you and your wonderful man.

Jacqui: I was waiting for him to call one night to let me know what time he'd be coming home, and he didn't. When he got home, I said something like, "You didn't call. What's happening? You didn't let me know what's going on," and he was extremely apologetic. He had left me a message much earlier in the day saying, "Yeah, I'm going to be home in a few minutes," so in his mind, he thought he had called, but it ended up being a couple of hours, so for me, I'm thinking, "Gosh, is he all right? Did he die in an accident?" He said, "I'm so sorry to have made you worry."

A wonderful man is quick to apologize. After all, he never intends to hurt you.

Melody: A quality I really appreciate about my husband is that he's extremely forgiving. If there's a situation where he wouldn't necessarily even have done something wrong, he's so quick to apologize, which I think is his humility. He doesn't have to. I think he's very conscious to say, "I'm sure there's a part I play in whatever it is we're doing, and I'm sorry for whatever that is." I see it play out in his life in a lot of ways. He is extremely forgiving in how he relates to everyone—a boss or another parent or the people he supervises.

He works with junior high students, and one girl was mad at him for getting her in trouble for her bad behavior. He met with the girl and her mother later that day. Even though she was obviously in the wrong, he said right away, "I'm very sorry that I hurt your feelings in any way." He did not have to do that. She, not him, caused her own problems. She did not respect his authority. He could easily have said, "You need to change your attitude and if you don't . . ." He realizes that even if you do things right, people's feelings can be hurt.

A wonderful man's attitude of apology and forgiveness extends to others in his life as well as you. Some women may feel that a man is weak or soft for apologizing when he hasn't obviously done anything wrong. ("Real men don't say they're sorry.") In fact, the reverse is true; it takes great inner strength as well as compassion to care about our impact on others.

Lucy: What I appreciate most about my husband is his ability to forgive quickly. He's really taught me how to forgive. It amazed me from the very beginning, and I've really grown to value that in a relationship. I have a bit of a temper, and usually I'm first to leave the room. Even in a typical mundane argument, I will leave the room in a huff and go to our bedroom. He'll knock on the door and say, "I'm really sorry. I just spoke too soon. I jumped off the deep end. I'm sorry." He's very patient, because sometimes it takes more than that one time for me to say, "Okay, honey, I forgive you too." It can take several efforts on his part to get me to forgive and to settle down and be willing to work it out. He'll be patient with me. I really appreciate that, because I need that in a relationship.

One of the things I love is that he will leave me little notes all over the place. If I'm having a rough day, I'll find these notes that say, "Hang in there, honey, it's going to get better." He really wants to work things out, wants us to be happy, and he does a lot for that to happen.

A wonderful man wants your forgiveness as much as he wants to forgive and will do what it takes to come to that.

Anne: My husband struggled with anger for a large part of the seventeen years we've been married, and it was because "he's Greek." He tied everything about himself to his Greek heritage. He was intense because he was Greek. He liked to cook because he was Greek. He liked olive oil because he was Greek. It was like, "Okay, I get it. You're Greek." And this anger problem he had, well, that was because he was Greek too. And I had to accept it because he was Greek. It was a nationalistic thing. And I knew he was this great guy overall, but he justified his less wonderful aspects with his nationality. I had always had a really strong personality until I got married. Then I became this little wimp of a woman. I didn't know how to stand up to his temper when he'd get angry and yell at me. It became this thing that was bigger than me. And I became a little mouse.

Then one day my husband went to a seminar and woke up. He realized that his anger had nothing to do with being Greek—that truly he was an angry man and furthermore that he was mistreating his wife, emotionally abusing me with his anger. And he came home in tears and fell on his face in front of me. He begged for forgiveness, and he hasn't been the same husband since. Not just that one day, but every day since then he has really tried to be a new man.

I just appreciate him so much for that. He was over forty years old when he came to this realization. For over forty years, he had been an angry man. They talk about how long it takes to develop a habit, so, I mean, he'd been practicing anger for a long time. I just think how much love it takes to practice not being an angry man, but instead a loving, kind man to me. He practices being patient and considerate of me, every day. Every once in a while, he'll get mad again, and after, he will come to me and say, "I'm so sorry, I'm so sorry." He asks me to keep an eye on his temper, because he doesn't want to be that man again. We will see couples when we're out, and if he sees someone being sharp with his wife, he'll say, "Is that what I was like?" And I'll say, "Yeah," and he'll say, "Oh, gosh, I am so sorry." It just means the world to me that he loved me enough to want to change. I used to walk around cowering in my shame all day long. But now I can walk around and be myself. I can be a whole woman. I can be Anne. I can be who I really am.

A wonderful man will back up his "I'm sorry" with behavior that demonstrates that his apology is genuine. He will not allow his bad behavior to continue.

Anger is a challenge for many of us. It can easily tip into outright abuse. Had Anne's husband not become aware of his temper and taken strong measures to curtail his anger, she may have ended up a victim of abuse. However, Anne's husband was essentially a good man. He was honest, reliable, trustworthy, responsive, responsible, appreciative of other people, and caring. He had none of the hallmarks of an abusive individual (see the appendix). He did, however, have a quick temper. He would flare up at minor annoyances and yell. He got away with it because he attributed his explosions to his passionate Greek nature, and others accepted this characterization. His temper took its toll on Anne, however, as she became "a little mouse of a woman." Fortunately, her husband attended a seminar that changed all that. He blossomed into a wonderful man through the acceptance of his anger as a problem—his problem—and he took immediate and effective steps to resolve the situation. Along with that, he showed sincere remorse and asked for forgiveness.

Should you find yourself in a relationship with an otherwise good but quick-tempered man, there's no need to wait for a seminar or some other outside influence to change your partner's anger habit. When you first witness an outburst, wait until the two of you are in a calm mood and then ask him in a matter-of-fact, neutral tone what hurt or bothered him to set him off. If indeed it's something that might disturb anybody, let your partner know that you understand that what happened annoyed him, but that his anger is frightening and this behavior is not healthy for either of you. It certainly is not conducive to the well-being of your relationship.

If your man can hear you and is willing to accept responsibility for his temper, you may be able to continue in the relationship successfully. You can develop a time-out signal for each other, like the time-out sign used in sports, to cut short any outbursts. Agree with your mate that when you make that sign, everything has to stop right then. Once you've made the time-out sign, calmly let him know that you need to take a break. You're going to take a walk or a bath, or just go into another room—whatever works for you.

If, however, what set him off is not understandable to you, or if he does not take responsibility for his anger, it's imperative to get professional help as soon as possible. Similarly, if he cannot deal appropriately with his outbursts despite the best efforts of both of you, you should seek help. It is not acceptable for you to live in an atmosphere of fear. It will ruin your relationship.

May: My husband really knows how to work at a marriage. He's learned that from his parents, I think. We love each other so much. He's constantly looking out for me, for my benefit. Talk about forgiveness! When we were first married,

I would give him the silent treatment. But it wouldn't work, because it would seem like he was having a great time without me. So I'm on the couch, upset, pretending to be asleep, and meanwhile he's playing with the kids or watching TV, having a great time. So I'd have to go over and apologize to him. And he'd always be quick to forgive me—just like he'd be quick to apologize if he thought he'd done something. I learned that a good marriage takes communication, and I discovered the good things communication leads to.

True forgiveness requires communication, and a wonderful man is always willing to communicate.

A WONDERFUL MAN doesn't play mind games. He's a straight shooter. If you're miffed at him, you'd better tell him, because he's not going to wait around, trying to guess what's going on with you. He will, as Danielle's husband does, ask, "Did I do something wrong?" or "Have I offended you?" but if you lie through your teeth and say no, and then go silent on him, he'll take your no at face value and leave you to your pout.

So when May would dish out the silent treatment to her husband during the first years of their marriage, he would ignore it and simply go about his day. Lataesha's husband was always willing to apologize and work things through, which finally made her silent treatment ineffective. Lucy's husband would wear her silent treatment down with his own ready apologies. Danielle's husband would make himself available for discussion, and when she refused it, let her know he was ready whenever she was.

My, but this does upset our manipulative applecart! We are used to men, from our fathers on through boyfriends and husbands, yielding to the power of the silent pout. It's quite a shock when someone doesn't. And yet it's good when our pouts fail, because genuine emotional intimacy cannot exist in a relationship fueled by power struggles. That's what the silent treatment is: a power struggle. By withholding your love, you are trying to force your man to cower before you, admit you're right, and come crawling back. You are hoping he'll do anything to restore that state of love he enjoys so much. But your wonderful man has perfect faith in that love. He also has great faith in you. He actually believes what you tell him. When you say there's nothing that you're angry about and nothing he can do, he trusts that you will work through whatever angst you're experiencing and return to him as your usual happy, loving self.

You can't engage in power struggles and be forgiving at the same time. These are mutually exclusive behaviors. You get to choose: you can adopt a "my way or the highway" approach to disagreements and upsets, maintaining, "I'm right, you're wrong," until death do you part. Or you can recognize that disagreements and upsets are an opportunity to get to know each other better, to gain respect for each other's point of view, and thus to strengthen an already blessed relationship.

That's why wonderful men are so quick to apologize and to forgive. They recognize that who's right isn't the point; we're all fallible, we all make mistakes, and we all hurt those we love without meaning to. They want to get on to the good part: understanding each other better so the love can grow in breadth and depth. Lucy's husband is quick to knock on their bedroom door and say, "I'm sorry," for whatever part he may have played. Melody's husband apologizes even when he doesn't know what went wrong, for he understands that humans err and he's willing to be accountable. May's husband is quick to apologize if he thinks he's done something and quick to forgive. Anne's husband will make the choice to forgive even when he knows he isn't wrong.

The Ladies point out in their stories how much their husbands have helped them become forgiving. Lataesha, Lucy, May, and Danielle all speak of how their wonderful men set a precedent for forgiveness by their willingness to apologize and forgive. Our relationships can only benefit from such humility. That's what forgiveness is all about: the humble acknowledgment of our common humanity.

Forgiveness comes in small packages as well as large. The way Linda happily forgives her husband for forgetting to take out the trash shows how valuable a sense of humor is in the practice of forgiveness. As Linda so accurately stated, "Life's too short," and much of the grief we give each other in relationships is over things too petty to matter. We bedevil each other over the trash and the toothpaste cap and other trivialities, mostly because we're so invested in our belief that we are right, at great cost to the joy in our relationships. A wonderful man just won't be interested in getting involved in that type of power struggle, so why not give it up and see the humor in our foibles?

Forgiveness truly is a choice. Nothing says you must harbor pain and resentment in your heart. You have to make an effort either way: it takes energy to maintain the pain, just as it takes energy to release it. Hanging on to a hurt doesn't make it go away. If anything, since whatever you focus on grows, hanging on to the hurt simply amplifies it.

You may think that by hanging on to the hurt, you are punishing the one who hurt you and giving him what he deserves, but in truth, you're only prolonging your own suffering, not just your emotional and mental pain, and also endangering your physical health and well-being. Research has demonstrated repeatedly how nursing resentment and keeping anger alive inside you are linked to cancer and the suppression of our immune systems. No less an authority than Dr. Vicki Rackner, a board-certified surgeon and clinical instructor at the University of Washington's School of Medicine, reminds us that the health consequences of anger and resentment are comparable to those of smoking. As to your immune system, that critical front line of defense, the more suppressed your immune system, the less your body is able to protect itself against any and all ills. Hanging on to the hurt can hurt you deeply. And what use is punishment in a relationship anyway? The object of a relationship is joy, not pain. That's why wonderful men are wise when they don't buy into our silence or noisier attacks of temper. They know that only by talking things through and dealing with the hurt openly together can healing take place. The American Institute for Preventive Medicine sums it up neatly: "Avoid blaming the other person. This puts him or her on the defensive and prevents communication. When blaming starts, listening stops" (*Minding Your Mental Health*, 5th edition, 2004).

Yet forgiveness can be hard. It doesn't come easily or naturally for many of us. Our survival instincts rush to the fore, and we defend ourselves from the hurt by separating ourselves emotionally, even physically, from the person who wounded us. At the extreme, we seek revenge. Forgiveness requires empathy—the willingness to step into the other person's shoes, to see what led to their hurtful action, to listen to their perspective on what happened. There's little chance of empathy when you are stung by his forgetting your birthday again, or finishing the shampoo when he knew that you had an important meeting this morning, or leaving you adrift at his company party while he flirts with every woman in the room. How can you put yourself in his shoes when you'd never do any of those things? And forgive him? Why? *He's* the one who should be begging forgiveness from *you*.

Your anger is your psyche's way of protecting you from the wound to your self-respect, your self-esteem. There's a nagging little voice inside that says, consciously or not, "You're not worth much, are you, if he can forget your birthday and ignore your needs? Heck, you're of so little value to him that he can ignore you and pay court to whatever female catches his eye." It hurts too much to hear these demeaning thoughts about ourselves, so we defend ourselves by projecting all the bad feelings out there onto him. *He's* the unworthy one; *he's* the one too insignificant to be cared about. Forgive *him?* In his dreams!

But although it might seem that forgiveness is for his benefit, an act of concession to him, it is above all for *your* benefit. Only forgiveness will assuage the hurt you feel. Only forgiveness will release you from your anguish and anger and restore your emotional well-being and positive sense of self. Forgiveness has great health benefits as well. Studies from respected institutions such as Duke University and the Mayo Clinic show that forgiveness has a beneficial effect on your blood pressure and heart rate: people who forgive others experience lower levels of pain, anger, and depression.

Some may think that forgiving is a sign of weakness. On the contrary, it takes a strong and courageous person to counter the instinctive push toward self-defense and vindication and to say instead, "I know I am a worthy person. I know I am a valuable human being. I can make the effort to understand why my mate hurt me." It takes a strong and courageous person to understand that forgiveness is not condoning. It is not approving of what the other did, excusing or justifying his behavior. Forgiveness is not letting him off the hook, and it is not brushing the event aside with, "Never mind, it's nothing, it's over." It is not minimizing or denying or in any way excusing your hurt or your feelings.

And forgiveness is most decidedly not the same as forgetting. What happened happened, and that must be dealt with. Forgiveness is an acknowledgment of our common humanity, of the imperfections we are all heir to. It is a willingness to see things from the other's point of view, to understand that the other's actions have legitimacy in their mind—whether you agree with them or not. Forgiveness is a willingness to see things new, to go forward with a better understanding of each other. As difficult as it may sometimes be, forgiveness is what allows us imperfect humans to engage in intimate relationships of depth and substance. Forgiveness allows couples to develop happy, healthy relationships despite the fact that we all, usually inadvertently, at some time or another cause our partners emotional pain.

Forgiveness, when approached in this way, is a choice to better understand each other to the benefit of the relationship. Forgiveness means you look past the act and at the person. You consider who your mate is as a whole; you put the act or behavior in the larger context of what you know to be true about your mate. It is what psychologists, among them Dr. Ellen Langer of Harvard University, with her extensive research on mindfulness, mean when they talk about how behavior is interpreted and understood differently depending on the perspective from which it is viewed. Putting yourself in your mate's place, seeing the situation from his point of view, allows you to understand what he did differently. That understanding is frequently the key to forgiveness, and forgiveness is a necessary step forward if the relationship is to thrive.

When Anne's husband understood what his anger had done to his wife, how it had diminished her self-esteem and self-worth, he was profoundly distressed, and from that day forward, he made every effort to treat her with tenderness and set aside his long-standing habit of anger. Anne not only forgave him but appreciated what this change in habit meant for him. She understands what this effort must have cost her man in the greater scheme of his life. Her understanding and appreciation in addition to her forgiveness is what supports her wonderful man's ability to keep that effort up. Another woman might not have been so forgiving and thought, "Too little, too late," or, "Yeah, right. We'll see how long this lasts." But Anne accepted the change as real and supported it with courage and profound compassion. She let go of the past without blame or any attempt at vindication. She is an inspiration.

Often what stops us from forgiving is the fear that forgiveness represents a backward step in the relationship: "If I forgive him, he'll think it's okay with me and just do it again." That may be true when you're dealing with an abusive individual, but not when you're dealing with a good person. The key is the communication that occurs in the process of forgiving. That communication—the coming to an understanding of why each of you did what you did and reacted as you did—is what makes forgiveness real, not just some pat "I'm sorry" that you utter robotically.

Forgiveness also means giving up the defensive posturing so many of us assume by assigning blame: "He's the one who messed up. It wasn't my fault." "He started it!" "I'm not the one who . . ." When you defend against something, you push away your mate. You have to separate from him in order to lay all the blame on him and keep yourself unsullied. Pushing away in this manner damages the bond between you and reinforces "I'm me" and "you're you" at the cost of "we're us." Defensiveness is what Dr. John Gottman identifies as the third of the "Four Horsemen of the Apocalypse"—the warning signs of a marriage thundering toward disaster. Dr. Gottman's cutting-edge research put couples in a laboratory situation where their every word, gesture, and utterance was videotaped and then analyzed extensively. His two decades of research demonstrate undeniably what forces rip apart a marriage, starting with criticism that involves blame (as opposed to nonblaming complaining, which is healthy), progressing into contempt (you disdain the one you blame), which triggers defensiveness, finally leading to shutting out your mate entirely.

Body language is very indicative of what's going on in a relationship. When I see a couple sitting as far apart as possible from each other on the couch in my therapy office, I know immediately that one partner is blaming the other for something, or they're both blaming each other. The blame interferes with everything else going on in their lives, and if they can't resolve the issue, they won't just edge to opposite sides of the couch—they'll separate entirely. Blame makes a poor bed partner.

A good example of this is one couple in which the wife resented her husband's frequent socializing with friends, accusing him of being callous and uncaring of her needs. Her husband retorted that he liked to socialize and she could come along whenever she wanted. The wife snapped back that being the only wife in a group of a dozen other guys, all single, was the true definition of a fifth wheel. Why couldn't he grow up, accept that he wasn't a single guy anymore, and behave like a "normal" married man? The husband blamed his wife for wanting to cage him in: surely she knew how social he was before she married him. Both husband and wife were absolutely unwilling to make an attempt to understand the other's point of view. They would not let go of the blame game they played so adeptly, and I watched sadly as they no longer even sat on the same couch, but appropriated separate chairs, and, soon after, separated entirely.

If unresolved, blame pervades your entire relationship. It takes over, occupying all of your emotional energy, making it impossible to see your partner as anything but the perpetrator of harm. Psychological studies of blame show that people are most likely to blame those whose behavior confirms unfavorable expectations. As you let your blame fester, and continue to see your partner through the lens of your hurt and resentment, you define more and more of what he does as in some way defective and thus blameworthy. What you expect is what you get. The healthy underpinnings of the marriage—trust, open communication, caring—are eroded. Who wants to trust a person who is causing you harm? Few of us qualify as genuine masochists. Certainly in the moment, it feels good to put the burden of your misery on somebody else's shoulder. It restores the balance of power. By blaming your partner, you feel less like a victim. The roles have been reversed. You now feel morally superior—"He done me wrong"—and can assert your righteousness. After all, nothing you did or said warranted his bad behavior. Right? You feel in control once more as you condemn your man's behavior, letting him know just how wrong and hurtful he was.

This is why we often hold on to grudges, bringing them up in totally unrelated arguments years later. We use past hurts to reestablish our sense of power and reassert our moral superiority when a current issue threatens our self-esteem. It never really works, though. All that blaming and holding on to grudges does is perpetuate bad feelings in the present, eroding the good feelings you and your mate have toward each other. Studies show that blaming one's spouse for marital problems is directly related to marital dissatisfaction. Generally speaking, blaming others interferes with your ability to come up with effective ways to cope with the situation. You're less likely to respond in positive ways to your partner. Blame and resentment separate you from each other rather than draw you closer together. Think about it: Would you like to cuddle up to someone who thinks you're to blame for all his misery? Hardly. Blaming never really makes anybody feel good. It may temporarily numb your pain in a big dose of self-pity, but it never makes you joyous and happy.

Some of us blame in another way: you may blame yourself entirely for whatever happened. This isn't very satisfying, either. "It's all my fault" isn't any more conducive to restoring the goodness between you than "It's all your fault." Research demonstrates that spouses who engage in more self-blame may tend to have an increased risk of depression, and being depressed isn't good for you or your relationship. As psychologists tell us (and we know from our own experience), depression is most frequently expressed as shutting down the self, turning inward. You're more likely to withdraw from your mate or not engage in problem solving. Turning inward may have its benefits—introspection is often what precedes change—but in the end, turning outward toward your mate is what will facilitate the necessary conversation that allows forgiveness and, with it, restores your love.

Whether you blame yourself or your partner, letting go of blame is the road to putting past hurts and injustices where they belong: in the past. It redefines both you and your man as worthy individuals, neither one of you victims, each endowed with personal power— power that is used not to beat each other down but to build each other up, to nourish each other's lives. It puts each of you back in control of your own lives, no longer making choices based on rehashing old pain.

Most important, neither blaming your mate nor blaming yourself solves whatever problem engendered the upset in the first place. In addition, blaming hampers the forgiveness process as everyone scurries around trying to preserve whatever personal dignity they can. Instead of wasting your energies blaming, engage the forgiveness process by focusing on accountability and responsibility.

Accountability is your willingness to assess which part of the problem belongs to you and which part to your mate. Responsibility is your willingness and ability to respond to that for which you are accountable. The conversation that needs to take place so that forgiveness is genuine is one in which you examine together your respective accountability ("this is how I contributed to the situation") and responsibility ("this is how I responded to the situation") and sort out what amends need to be made this time, or how you'd like to do it differently next time.

We frequently resist being accountable and responsible because we fear that we'll be held accountable for too much, or for aspects of the problem that were never in our control. For example, the wife whose husband socialized more than she liked was asked by her husband to accept that she contributed to the situation by marrying him knowing he was social. Her accountability, according to him, was, "Like it or lump it." This was not only unfair in the attribution of accountability, but it was imposed unilaterally rather than discovered through discussion between husband and wife. A good man won't impose one-way accountability. He'll be sufficiently honest and caring to discuss his part as well as yours. A good man becomes a wonderful man as you are willing to engage in discussions of accountability and responsibility, more invested in coming to genuine forgiveness than you are in hanging on to your position, however righteous you may feel.

When you consent to a medical procedure, you're asked to give informed consent, meaning that you understand what the procedure is for, what the consequences may be, and so on. If consent isn't informed, it's not consent: you don't know what you're consenting to. Think of discussions about accountability and responsibility as a way to arrive at informed forgiveness. If your forgiveness isn't informed, it may be difficult to feel that your forgiveness is true. Have the courage to talk the situation through until both of you feel you have a solid understanding of what happened, what amends need to be made, if any, and what steps should be taken to avoid future mishaps.

A wonderful man will be there with you and for you, all the way. As you are honest and straightforward with each other, willing to work through hurts and disappointments without pointing fingers and posturing to defend yourselves, you'll find that forgiveness comes easily, leaving more room for joy and love in your hearts.

Week #5 of Your 35 Days to a Wonderful Man: Days 21–25

This week you'll:

Quit pulling the silent treatment on your man.
Be the first to apologize.
Give up your "I'm right, you're wrong" position.
Be accountable for your part in whatever problems occur.
Forgive genuinely.

Day 21: Today I'll quit pulling the silent treatment on my man.

Today you'll quit pulling the silent treatment on your man. Period. End of sentence; end of behavior. This may be the most radical change you will make, for so many of us have practiced the silent treatment since birth. Variations on this behavior are the instant cry, where you burst into tears the moment something distresses you, or the instant yell, where you yell and scream the moment something distresses you. What these three behaviors have in common is they stop all communication. They make resolving the upset and moving on virtually impossible. Today, quit whichever one is your perennial fallback. You will no longer use silence, tears, or lashing out to manipulate your man into submission. Dedicate yourself to open and honest communication no matter how painful or unfamiliar it is. It will get easier and downright comfortable with practice.

Day 22: Today I'll be the first to apologize.

Today you will use phrases like, "I'm sorry that what I did or said hurt you; it wasn't my intention," and, "I'm sorry I upset you." Apology is much easier when you understand that you are first and foremost apologizing for hurting your man, not apologizing for your opinion or your behavior. That's why you don't have to wait to apologize. You're not admitting your opinion or behavior was wrong; you're expressing your distress at upsetting your mate. The sooner you can do that, the sooner you can engage in the honest communication that will allow you to resolve what caused the upset in the first place. Today, commit to being the first to apologize whenever there's an upset. You'll make it easier for your man to be wonderful in return.

Day 23: Today I'll give up my "I'm right, you're wrong" position.

Today you'll foreswear your righteousness, as reluctant as you may be to do so. There's no forgiveness in saying, "I'm right, you're wrong," and this position doesn't leave room for a true relationship. "I'm right, you're wrong" divides you into "you" and "me," leaving behind any hope of "us." "I'm right, you're wrong" stomps on any possibility of working things through, and a wonderful man will always want to work things through. Step off your "I'm right" pedestal and meet your man at, "We have different ways of seeing and doing things, and sometimes they collide. Let's talk." Today observe how many times you think, "I'm right, you're wrong," about your man, whether you verbalize it or not. Jot down these instances if it helps you see your righteousness. Decide you won't do that anymore. When you feel the urge come on, take a deep breath and say to yourself, "Different. Not right or wrong. Different," and let that mantra help you stay steady on course.

Day 24: Today I'll be accountable for my part in whatever problems occur.

As tempting as it is to believe you could do no wrong, the problems between two people always involve a share of responsibility and accountability on both sides. True, sometimes it may seem the larger share is the other person's, but what's important isn't the size of your part; it's that you are accountable. Look back on your last couple of upsets. How were you accountable? Or not? Be unflinching in your self-examination. Don't justify your behavior. Today, have the courage and integrity to be accountable for your part in any distress or upset. Explore what you contributed to the situation and how you responded. Determine what you need to do differently next time. Make whatever amends are appropriate. Don't shy away from accountability. It is a major step toward true empowerment. Your accountability encourages your man's accountability, and with it, more of his wonderfulness.

Day 25: Today I'll forgive genuinely.

Too often, our "I forgive you" is given grudgingly, halfheartedly. We don't really mean it, but we say it so the argument won't go on and on, or because we're afraid of what will happen if we don't (He'll leave? Divorce me? Go off with his arm candy?). Today, forgive genuinely. Recognize that forgiving doesn't mean condoning. It doesn't mean you accept or like whatever it was he did. Forgiving means you recognize he's human and makes mistakes, just like you do. However, this won't work if you haven't had sufficient conversation, so today, commit to talking things through until you understand why he did what he did, how you contributed to it, and how you both can do things differently in the future. Look back on something you still haven't forgiven him for in this different light. Anything you can't figure out by yourself, talk over with your man. Now, forgive. Your heart will be in it this time. And now you have a template for genuine forgiveness you can use time and time again.

Use the weekend to repeat whichever of the days were more challenging for you.

Keep track of your progress daily on your "How Did I Do Today?" chart. Enter check marks to keep track of how you did: one check for "Yes, I did," two checks for "Yes, I really did," or three for "I was brilliant on this one!" and either a minus or zero if you didn't do the item. You'll be able to see at a glance how you're doing.

Remember to keep practicing the past weeks' items as you go forward with this week's plan.

How Did I Do Today?

Days 21–25

Item	Day 21	Day 22	Day 23	Day 24	Day 25	SAT	SUN
Did I quit pulling the silent treatment on my man?							
Was I the first to apologize?							
Did I give up my "I'm right, you're wrong" position?							
Was I accountable for my part in whatever problems occurred?							
Did I forgive genuinely?							

To forgive is to set a prisoner free and discover that the prisoner was you.

LEWIS B. SMEDES, *professor of theology and ethics*

CHAPTER 6

RULES OF ENGAGEMENT: TOGETHERNESS

A WONDERFUL MAN is a partner.

A wonderful man is more than someone you're in love with who's in love with you (as fantastic as that is). A wonderful man is someone who enjoys being actively engaged with you, in your life, in your relationship, with your family—in all that matters to you.

A wonderful man doesn't sit on the sidelines, letting you "do" your life as he goes about "doing" his. He is involved; he participates. He will give you honest and loving feedback and expects the same in return. A wonderful man is your life partner in the fullest, richest meaning of the term, as you are his.

Melia: My husband is truly always there for me no matter what my needs are. When we were first dating, I got sick with the flu and was bedridden for a week. He lived at that time in Hacienda Heights, and I lived in the heart of West LA. The guy I dated before my husband lived much closer to me than Hacienda Heights, but felt it was too far to make the drive, so I saw him only once a week—and this went on for over a year. But my husband, who I'd been dating for only three weeks, found out that I was sick and drove from his work in Monterey Park to his home, picked up his children, went to the market, and bought the biggest bottle of vitamin C I have ever seen in my life, cold medicine, and a bag of throat lozenges. He showed up at my door with this care package! Boy, was I surprised! He had driven all that way just to try to make me feel better—and one way was 30.3 miles. That really meant a lot to me. He didn't have to do that—I really did have everything that I needed—but to go to that distance for me was just exceptional. He really had my heart then. I knew that if he would go to that effort to surprise me, then he would be there for me, always. And twenty-one years later, he is.

It doesn't matter if you're in bed with a negligee or with the flu, a partner will want to be there with you, for you.

May: It's like a dance. We always love to do things together. I found out he loved to watch basketball, so I learned the game so I could spend the time watching basketball with him on Sundays. When he started playing golf, he asked me, "Would you go take some lessons too, so we can go on the golf course and play together?" and we did that. And then he knows that I like to try different things, different kinds of foods, and although he's never been exposed to that, he's kept an open mind. He'll go out and try new things with me, and he tries to enjoy the stuff that I enjoy, so we can spend time together. That's just so precious.

True partners participate actively in each other's lives.

Melody: My husband is a really good listener to me. I'm a talker. I always have a lot to say, and he's always there to listen to me. We love to dream together. I appreciate that—because as we do it, we get to know each other better, and we give each other purpose to do things.

The operative word in partnership is *together*—things done, dreamed, lived together.

Olivia: When we were first dating, there were a few moments when I said to myself, "Wow, what a guy." One Sunday morning, we'd cooked up this great big breakfast together. As we sat down to eat it, I said, "I'm hot"—with all the cooking, the kitchen had heated up—and without a word, he got up and started opening windows. He didn't even say, "Oh, you are," or anything. He just did something about it. I thought, "Wow, that's really cool."

Another time, we were going to do something, and I said, "I have my period"—because I did—and his response was, "Oh, are you okay? Do you feel okay?" and this really struck me. I had been in a relationship where the guy didn't get that at all. And another time, we were browsing in a bookstore, and I was looking at a novel that I thought looked interesting. But then I put it down and didn't buy it. The next time I saw him, he brought the novel with him. All these things told me this guy was for real.

A partner is one who engages in your day-to-day, not just his own.

Mercedes: I'm constantly on the go. And what matters is keeping my husband in the loop, and letting him know what's going on with everything I'm involved in. Every time I get home, he asks, "So what happened? Is everything going okay with so-and-so?" He's interested to know. When we go to a party, he'll stay there for hours talking to someone just because he's interested in people's lives and really will listen. He genuinely cares.

A wonderful man enjoys engaging, and he will be your partner to the extent that you involve him in your life.

Jacqui: I love the fact that my husband loves to shop with me. When we go look for stuff, he'll give me his input and get really involved. I love knowing that he enjoys it, that he's putting some of himself into the shopping experience.

A wonderful man partners you willingly in whatever aspect of life you invite him to.

Mercedes: My husband gives me feedback on how to handle certain situations if I'm having a problem. I'm going to be the maid of honor for my friend Jessica soon, but I've been having drama with the bride's family over who's taking care of what—like the rehearsal dinner, the bridal shower, and all that. So Eddie has been very encouraging, really talking it out and suggesting things, like, "Well, maybe you need to support Jessica in what she wants and tell the family you're taking care of all the aspects of the bridal shower so they don't have to worry about it." He'll say things like, "Well, this is what you're dealing with, with this person," which helps me a lot because for some reason he has a better grasp of personalities. He's able to see things I don't notice. So it's great to know that I can say, "This is what's going on. What do you think?" and get his feedback.

A partner is someone who helps you work things out for yourself.

Lani: I grew up in a family where we rarely heard, "I love you." My parents loved us kids, but they didn't say it much. So I tend not to be verbally affectionate either. My husband knows that my upbringing is why I don't verbalize my affection or appreciation much, and he will tell me when he doesn't feel he or the kids are being appreciated. He'll say, "I really feel you don't appreciate me for what I've done," and that cues me to say, "You know, you're right. I need to think about it, and that's true." Sometimes he'll even say that that I need to focus on the kids more, appreciate and praise them more openly. And so it's nice that he knows my weaknesses and isn't afraid to say, "You know, you need to do this more because I think our daughter is feeling . . ."

A true partner helps you grow without ever putting you down.

Grace: It's the little things. I absolutely hate emptying the dishwasher. With the size of my family (six kids) there is a lot to empty, and just keeping the house running and everything going, picking up after everybody, is a lot of work. Five minutes after I've finished cleaning and tidying, everything's a mess again. And my husband knows that, and he doesn't mind, and every chance he gets he picks things up. I appreciate that so much. He'll give the kids a bath without my asking. He'll thank me for making dinner, when I think, "Well, that's my job."

Then for my thirtieth birthday, when I was dealing with three kids under the age of four, he threw me a surprise party, which he had to do without my help. He enlisted my friends and family as best he could, but it was his initiative. He did all the planning, got everything organized, and even organized a three-day trip to Carmel as my birthday gift. The most amazing thing that he does, when he knows I need it, is to take me out of my role as mother and put me back into my role as wife. He'll say, "Honey, we need a date night. Let's you and I go do this." He won't let me do one more bit of work. He protects me in that sense too.

When a wonderful man is your partner, he puts your well-being and happiness on a par with his own.

Linda: It's my duty to walk the dogs and take care of them. I don't want them to be a burden for my husband, since they were mine before we got married. I'll ask him in the morning if he wants to walk with me and the dogs, and he'll say, "No, I'm sleepy," and I'm cool with that since I don't expect it. On Saturday mornings, I know he likes to sleep in, so I'm very quiet when I get up. Then I'll hear the door shut upstairs, and Jack will come down the stairs. I'll say, "What are you doing?" and he'll say, "I'm coming with you on the walk," just because he knows that I love it. It's a little thing, but I appreciate it so much and let him know it.

A week ago he was out of town on a business trip, and he changed his flight to come home a day early without my knowing about it. When I got home, he was already there, and it was so exciting that he had come home early. It's those little things they do because they want to, not because they have to, that are so great.

A wonderful man seeks to involve himself in your life in ways that please you.

May: As a mom, you have to go shopping a lot. My husband didn't start out loving to shop. But I didn't want to go by myself, so he would go with me, and he's made it fun. He's really efficient. He'll ask me, "What are the sizes? What are the styles?" Things like that. And he's able to go to the clearance rack during sales and pull out stuff that I cannot find. All the different sizes make me dizzy. In the middle of all that chaos, he can find the right stuff for me and the kids. All these things he does for me are very precious.

A wonderful man doesn't participate grudgingly in your life. He does so with joy.

Julia: In his work, my husband deals with people all the time, and dealing with people is not always the easiest thing. One time I had five minutes left to get all sorts of things done to get our church choir together and then direct them for twenty-five minutes. This girl came up to me and said, "I can't sing with this person anymore. She comes late, she's always late, she doesn't know her part, she doesn't listen to her CDs, she doesn't know what to sing, she just messes me up." And I just didn't have time to talk with her thoroughly about the problem, so I just said, "Yeah, we've talked with her before; we'll deal with that." Really, I blew her off because I was feeling under pressure.

So when I came home, I talked to my husband about it. He listened and he said, "Okay, I can understand what you just went through, but let me tell you how you might have handled this just a little bit better," and he gave me some ideas as to how I might deal with a similar situation in the future. It was great because I never felt like he was telling me what to do because of the way he approached me about it: "How can I help her understand it in a way she's not going to feel I'm picking on her?" I could take it in and appreciate the help. It was great.

A partner is eager to help you with whatever you ask and will never demean or disrespect you in the process.

> **Lucy:** My mom and dad were married for twenty-one years, and then my dad up and left my mom for the church organist. It was really horrible. My dad got married again, had another family, moved on with his life. My mom was really hurt and very bitter. She swore she would never get married again. She'd say, "I don't trust men. I don't need them." Well, my mom comes over a lot to help with the kids, and because she lives alone and doesn't have a lot of people to talk to, she will talk to my husband. And he'll listen. Even if he has to go to work, he'll still listen. He's been doing this for eighteen years. Just a few months ago, my mom said, "Maybe it wouldn't be so bad to get married again," and I think my husband had a lot to do with that because of his relationship with her, his willingness to care for her. He always says, "Your mom just needs someone to listen to her, Lucy. She needs a man she can trust." She's come to believe that maybe not all men are cheating fools. I really appreciate that he's helped her in this way.

A wonderful man doesn't only participate in your life, he engages fully with those who are meaningful to you.

> **Lataesha:** Sometimes even among your girlfriends, it's hard to find a friend who's going to listen to you and really hear what it is you have to say. Well, it's even harder with men, because we communicate differently. When a woman needs to express whatever it is, whether it's telling a story or talking through her emotions, it's kind of hard to get men to understand what she needs right then. In the beginning, my

husband was very confused and would get frustrated because I would try to communicate very clearly—you know,
starting at the beginning and tying together everything in
between—but he would still be confused. Over time, I've
seen him actually try. He has made very deliberate attempts
over the years to understand what I say, really try to digest
what I'm talking about. Now our communication is so much
better. He'll say, "Okay, so this is what you're saying." And
then he'll know the moment when he should respond and
give his opinion, or to stay silent and leave something for
later. I'm so grateful to him for that. To have a husband listen
to you and really make the effort to understand you, to hear
where you're coming from, is something I really appreciate.

*A wonderful man will do what it takes to understand you, so as to
partner you better.*

Lani: We did a lot of talking before we got married. He was
open to that. He would communicate things to me, and I to
him. When we knew that we would probably get engaged,
we talked a lot about family issues—how many children each
of us was thinking of, what our professional goals were, our
personal desires. Communication played a really big part in
how we built our relationship.

He's German American and I'm Hawaiian Filipino. Because our relationship is multiracial, there were some issues
we had to deal with. I said to him, "I'm brown skinned. What
do you see in me?" and he said, "I see you. I don't see any
color." I so appreciate that in him. Still, our being from different backgrounds, different families, has affected our relationship. His family was very frugal with their money, while
I was brought up quite differently. I appreciate that we talk

about it. We can say to each other, "What is it that you don't like about how I deal with money?" This conversation is still going on after twenty-five years together. He thinks about me and where I come from, and I think about him and where he comes from, so that we can come to an understanding. That's what's made all the difference.

So much of being true partners is the willingness to be open and honest with each other, communicating with the interests of both equally in mind.

Linda: When we got married, I had never slept with a man before, but Jack had had sex. At first I was very insecure in that area. I would say, "I don't know what I'm doing, I have no clue." We came up with a solution that was really great for us that we used for a while at the beginning: a scoring system. It was on a ten-point scale, and we made it fun—you could never get below an 8.5, because just being together in an intimate way was great, and you never got more than a 9.9 because the 10 is the proverbial unachievable. When it was a 9.9 or a 9.8, we'd say, "Yeah, that was great! What was the best part for you?" Like the highlights. And when it was a lower score, we'd be like, "Yeah . . . ," and then we'd just talk about it. There were things I didn't know about anatomy, and it was great to get his feedback on it. It was so helpful—and it was all jovial, never hurtful or anything like that. And things would happen that would make us crack up and laugh hysterically. We'd talk about it later and laugh, like, "Remember when that happened! That was hilarious."

Partnering is a joy to a wonderful man, whatever aspect of your life it involves.

Jacqui: What comes out in our lovemaking is the acceptance of each other. It's not a performance thing. There's a real oneness between us that lets us really talk about stuff if it's not working right or whatever, or if he wants more intimacy or if I want more romance. Being able to go ahead and talk to him about those real intimate issues, these sensitive issues, means a lot to me.

Discussing your differences with a loving partner is just another way of coming to oneness.

Lani: My parents were very strict with us when we were growing up, and I basically raised my kids the way I was raised. My husband would work with me on this. He'd say, "Look at how you are dealing with the kids. This is how your family dealt with you kids—discipline—and remember how you felt." That would help me understand, and I would back off. I appreciate that he didn't blame or criticize me, but was just willing to sit down and talk about these things and work them through with me.

A wonderful man gives you feedback not to criticize you, but to work together and improve on what's important in your lives.

Lani: We had two babies, and then I had four miscarriages. My husband was with me through it all. I was depressed and couldn't understand why this was happening to me over and over again, but he was always by my side. He would be there, totally. He could sense when I was just going to break down, and he would nurture and take care of me. He would help me out with the children. He would take me out, or he would say, "You can't cook. Let's just go ahead and go out." He would see it through with me.

My husband has shown me time and time again how much he cares by being there for me when I'm down. I do the same for him. I spend a lot of time with my husband when I know he's down. My husband's a cardiologist, so he works a lot in stressful emergency situations, and he'll come home really tired, and I'll try to help him out by talking with him or getting him to go out, because I know he enjoys that. Or I'll spend time with the kids so he can get some time for himself.

With a wonderful man for your partner, you're never on your own— and neither is he.

Olivia: Starting with when we were dating, I always made a point of making my husband feel secure. I think it was because I have many different circles of friends, and I've always wanted the freedom to do what I wanted. I thought the way I could do that was to make him feel secure every time I came home. I would always make a point of saying, "I love you." I would tell him about everything that I did while I was out. If there were guys there, I'd let him know, and I'd say, "Oh, this guy tried to hit on me or whatever, but he was totally ridiculous." I would always be open about it. That way, even though I had a lot of different circles of friends, he was always a part of them. He was included in everything I did even when he wasn't there.

The more fully you include your wonderful man in your day, the more he can be a full partner in your life.

FOR A WONDERFUL man to be actively engaged in your life, you have to let him in. Many of us have grown so independent and self-sufficient that we hardly know how to allow someone else to get involved in our lives, or we've been so burned by bad prior experiences that we don't want to let someone in—look what a mess it caused last time! Our vulnerabilities can be intense. But a man has to be allowed to get involved, be engaged, and participate in your life if he is to reveal his wonderfulness. You can't get a partner without partnering.

The idea is not to hand over your life to a man. That's not partnership; it's abdicating your blessed individuality. Partners are people who dance together, figuratively or literally. Partners play on the same team. Partners share a game, a hope, a dream, a life.

Partnering, being engaged in each other's lives, can be thought of as the "doing" of love. It is love in action. Love, you see, is both a feeling and an action. You feel love for someone, you feel loved by someone, and that is marvelous, but for that love to have substance, it must be matched with loving actions. The feeling of love arises seemingly out of the blue. Who can explain why we fall in love with one person rather than another? The doing of love, however, is conscious, deliberate, and willful. Loving actions are fueled by choice. You choose to engage in your mate's life; you choose to allow his participation in your life.

Partnering brings you closer, makes your love more real, more solid. It makes you and your mate feel more fulfilled. Your relationship becomes deeper, more meaningful.

Letting your man know what's going on with you in your day-to-day life paves the way for him to be actively engaged in your life. Olivia recognized this early on and has always made a point of letting her then boyfriend, now husband, know where she had been, what she'd done, and with whom. Her boyfriend didn't require this of her; he had no need to control her. But Olivia chose to involve her boyfriend vicariously in her life so that he could participate in her experiences whether or not he was there. Mercedes too makes a point of letting her husband know what's up when he's not around—keeping him in the loop, as she says.

All of the Ladies clearly communicate to their men what's going on with them and what they want. Melia got her 30.3-mile vitamin C because she let him know she had the flu. Linda's husband joins her Saturday morning dog walk, something she cherishes. Windows open for Olivia when she feels too hot. Linda's sex life went from nonexistent to 9.9, Mercedes's husband goes shopping with her, and Lataesha's husband has become a dynamite listener.

Sometimes we believe that we shouldn't have to ask for what we want, that our men should be able to figure it out on their own. We spend so much of our time figuring out what others might want from us—our children, ailing family members, aging parents, even our pets—that we forget that our men may not have the same innate capacity (or need!) to read nonverbal signals. Harvard psychologist Robert Rosenthal's extensive research revealed that, in general, women are better at reading feelings from nonverbal cues. Dr. Judith Hall, professor of psychology at Northeastern University, came to a similar conclusion from her analysis of 125 studies on sensitivity: Women are generally better than men at figuring out the meaning of emotional messages. This is not particularly surprising, since the right brain—that side of the brain that women tend to use most—contributes largely to the expression of feelings as well as sensing or picking up on the emotions of others. We are biologically predisposed to intuiting what is going on with those around us; our mates are not.

This in itself would not pose a problem. But when we measure our partner's love for us by his ability to know instinctively what we want, problems emerge. Our predominantly right-brain orientation not only makes us more sensitive to what others are thinking and feeling, it also makes us more likely to take on a nurturing role, a quality reinforced by our socialized feminine roles. We tend to nurture those we care about. Your devotion to your child is usually greater than your care for an unrelated child; you spend sleepless nights caring for your elderly mother but are unlikely to show the same degree of concern for a neighbor's parent. When our mate doesn't just "know" what we want and provide it for us spontaneously, we think, "He doesn't care for me," because in our woman's world, we are extremely attuned to and nurturing of those we care most about. But this isn't necessarily the case for men.

Your mate's ability or inability to intuit what you want has little to do with his love for you. Maybe you think it's more valuable when your mate guesses what you want and produces it instantaneously. That might work in chick flicks, but it hardly ever does in real life. When you fail to communicate with your man about your emotional, mental, physical, and spiritual state, he can't be there for you. He doesn't know what to be there for! He's in the dark until you turn on the light. And you wonder why men don't step up to the plate more often!

What's worse about wanting our men to read our minds is that we then blame them for either not guessing what we want or guessing incorrectly. No matter what they do, men are on the losing end. Is it any surprise that men believe women are unfathomable, fickle mysteries and stop trying to understand? A wonderful man won't play that game. When you persist in not telling him what's up despite his willingness to engage with you, he'll walk away, and sooner rather than later. Compounding the problem is the fact that we just plain don't like to ask. In our culture, women are socialized to think first of others, not of themselves. It's often considered not "nice" or "ladylike" to state directly our wants and needs, since we're told we'll scare off a man with such behavior. Whether you believe that or not, you are influenced by this socialization. Many studies have been done in organizational and industrial psychology, the branch of psychology that deals with the work world, on the different ways men and women behave in the workplace and the attendant consequences— usually lower pay and fewer promotions for women whose intelligence, skill, and experience equal that of men.

These studies consistently find that the cause of this gender disparity in pay and promotions is that women don't like to ask. We feel that our work should speak for itself, and that pay and promotions should follow automatically. We don't like to ask, for a whole host of reasons, from how we are socialized as children to the cultural expectations of each gender, but the bottom line is that having to ask for something makes us feel insecure and uncomfortable. Too often, we don't feel we deserve whatever it is we want. After all, if we did, wouldn't it be granted automatically? Men, on the other hand, believe it is their responsibility to make sure they get what they deserve, and men have, generally speaking, great confidence that they deserve whatever it is they want. So men have far fewer qualms about asking.

Our men don't know it's hard for us to ask. They're not good at deciphering our nonverbal communications or indirect references. It is unfair and hurtful to require of them that they should be. Over time, as the Ladies' stories tell us, a wonderful man will make the effort, as you reveal yourself openly to him and ask for what you want directly, to be responsive to your wants and needs.

Some women might be tempted to keep their mates guessing, forgoing their mates' emotional security either because they think "it's none of his business," or because they believe that that mystery keeps the spice in the relationship. A game of "now you see me, now you don't" might be tantalizing when you're having an affair, but when you're working on a committed relationship—when you want the benefits and joys of partnering—that emotional distance is damaging. A wonderful man is ready and willing to give you all of himself. He's not going to settle for much less from you.

One of the benefits of partnering is honest and loving feedback that helps you through the challenging situations in life and helps you grow. A wonderful man will give you feedback in an appropriate and respectful way so that you can use it to your best advantage. When Mercedes asked her husband for his opinion on how she should deal with her friend's bridal party, he didn't say, "That's women's business. I haven't a clue," or laugh at her for getting worked up over it. Instead he gave it serious thought and offered a suggestion she valued. Julia felt perfectly comfortable letting her husband know that she wasn't pleased with how she'd handled the girl who didn't want to sing with another member of the group; she knew he wouldn't criticize or blame her actions or call her a dummy, but would help her figure out a better alternative for the future. Wonderful men aren't saints, but they don't label, they don't call you names, and they will do their best to offer their insight and support, which sometimes is a straightforward, "Gee, honey, I don't know."

When Lani's husband points out that she is repeating an old family pattern with her own children, he doesn't call her "stupid" or "insensitive" or say, "You're being a bitch." He simply reminds her of the pain such behavior had caused her and helps her find a different way of disciplining their kids. Another woman might take offense and say, "How dare you tell me how to deal with my kids!" and in the process lose the benefit of an engaged, participating, caring partner.

Partnering pays off when it comes to the more sensitive aspects of life. Think of how different it would have been for Linda if she had to go it alone in figuring out what makes for a satisfactory sexual experience, if she had to stumble through the intricacies of intimacy. Instead, she set aside whatever embarrassment or shame she may have felt at her sexual inexperience and engaged her man in helping the two of them together achieve sexual satisfaction. And Linda didn't blame her husband or criticize him for his depth of knowledge about sex. She could have gotten caught up in jealous thoughts of,

"Where did you learn that?" and "Who taught you how to do that?" Instead she just let her inexperience be what it was and laughed rather than cried.

Be willing to come to your man with whatever concerns or troubles you. A knight in shining armor needs to rescue the fair maiden, and even though you don't need rescuing, battling the dragon together rather than by yourself is a perk of partnering. A wonderful man wants to help you out whenever you ask. It is one of the primary characteristics of wonderful men. He loves helping out, but you do have to ask. A wonderful man will offer his opinion, never impose or force it on you, since he respects your ability to think for yourself and make good decisions for yourself.

It is critical to value and appreciate the feedback your man gives you, whether or not you agree with it or intend to implement it. What you're valuing first and foremost is the very act of giving you feedback—and, of course, you can appreciate the content of the feedback if you do indeed find it to be of value. With this, as with everything else, sincere appreciation is the only true appreciation.

A wonderful man will work things through with you. He won't expect you to do all the work of the relationship. He will want to be involved in making things better for the two of you, for your family.

Grace's husband doesn't just come home and retreat to the couch or the computer, oblivious to the six-kid chaos around him. He picks things up, gives the kids their baths, acknowledges his wife's contribution by thanking her for the most ordinary tasks, like making dinner. He behaves like a partner. Grace doesn't lambaste her husband with, "You're doing it wrong," or insinuate he couldn't possibly give the kids a bath properly, as we too often do. We don't realize how critical we are of the help we are offered. We don't realize that in criticizing how our mates do things, we drastically discourage them from helping out, from participating in the relationship.

A wonderful man will find many ways to improve things for your family. He will not only engage with you but will find ways to help appropriately with those who matter to you. Lucy's husband, for example, patiently listened to her mom for many years, teaching her mother that it's possible to trust a man. Another woman might have resented her husband's attentiveness to someone other than herself. She might have been jealous of the attention he gave her mom. That would have been most unfortunate. Stepping outside your own immediate needs and appreciating how your man helps others will reveal his wonderfulness in yet more delightful ways.

Doing things together is an important way of creating and sustaining partnership, whether it's cleaning up after the kids or getting involved in a hobby. May learned about basketball so she and her husband could watch games together, and he learned to try different kinds of food, one of May's pleasures, so the couple could experience culinary treats together. May learned to play golf and her husband learned to enjoy shopping in the interest of doing things together. Doing things together is one of the ways that wonderful men participate in the work of a relationship. If you take a look at long-term happy couples, you quickly see how much these men and women enjoy doing things together. We don't stop to think how separating our activities separates us emotionally as well as physically. Sure, there are some times you'd rather be with your girlfriends and he'd rather hang out with the guys, but for the most part, couples who choose to spend most of their time together are closer.

Part of being together is talking things over with each other and working through things together rather than attempting to figure everything out by yourself or hoping the issue will disappear if you ignore it. Lani's multiracial marriage thrives because she and her husband have talked—and talked and talked—about whatever dilemmas their cultural differences bring up. Her husband is open to discussing what she doesn't like about his choices, and she is open to listening to what her husband doesn't agree with about hers. The two of them have a common goal that allows them to rise above defending their own styles: achieving an understanding on which to found good decisions. That's partnering.

Entire bookshelves of excellent books have been written about the value of good communication in relationships. This is the basis of that working-things-through approach that wonderful men take to relationship difficulties. Be appreciative of your man's willingness to talk. Be open to his point of view and ideas for how to resolve the challenges life brings you. The more you allow his perspective and make efforts to see the value of his ideas, the more easily and readily your man can participate in making decisions, and the more mutual those decisions will be. Mutual decisions are always more satisfying and more likely to be implemented and succeed.

A wonderful man is awake and aware. He isn't just coasting along in the relationship, letting it carry him wherever. He pays attention to your needs and desires. He seeks to fill those needs or, at the very least, address them. A wonderful man feels good about making such efforts and is happy to continue to do so as long as he feels his efforts are making a difference in your life.

Don't be shy about acknowledging your man's responsiveness to your needs and wants. Let him know how much it means to you that he cares about your well-being, and doesn't just mouth his caring but actually does something about it. This is how you make it safe for your man to continue responding. His "gifts" are valued. He is not rejected. Indeed, in your eyes, he is worthy. His position as knight is secure. Few things feel better than being esteemed by your loved one.

If your man is to partner you, to dance with you, to share in all that you do, then you must in turn partner him. Too often we end up living side by side rather than together. We get wrapped up in our respective worlds and responsibilities: the kids, our work, community, family, church, errands, running the household—the list goes on. If your man doesn't volunteer information about his day, about what's going on at work or in his head, and seems pretty much okay, it may not even occur to you to ask questions about him and his well-being beyond the perfunctory "How's it going?" Let him know that you're interested! Remember the names of people or projects he's involved with, the situations that are of concern to him. Make an effort to stay current with what's going on in his life and with himself.

One reason a married man can become sidetracked by a woman at work is that his coworker is involved in his day-to-day life, knows what is of concern to him, and shares that concern. Such a partnership can easily deepen into love if the partnering aspect is missing at home.

You don't have to turn into your mate's secretary or associate to be involved in his day-to-day life. You need simply to demonstrate your sincere and active interest in your man's activities, whether they involve you or not. Just because your mate's accounting practice is boring to you doesn't mean that you can't remember the name of his favorite client or what's bugging him about his new assistant. You don't have to be a baseball fanatic to remember his favorite team and its latest victory.

Be a willing and enthusiastic helpmate when called on, whether it's to pick up a family gift for a birthday he forgot about or to run by the office store amid your errands and pick up that software he needs. When you're truly partners, he'll want to do the same for you when you're in a pinch. Be aware of his feelings, and be compassionate, encouraging, or validating, as the situation warrants. *Being there* isn't just a politically correct buzzword; it's an emotional reality—the sharing of each other's inner as well as outer lives.

Resist thinking, "He should remember to do things himself," or "He should be able to deal with it; he got himself into this situation in the first place." These thoughts only point out, yet again, his flaws. If you feel that you are giving more than he is, whether mentally, spiritually, physically, or emotionally, the time to bring it up is not when he's in a bind. Talk about it when you can sit down in a calm moment and work through it as you would any other concern.

Bear in mind that men call for help subtly. They do not wish to be seen as less than competent in your eyes. It's hard to be your knight in shining armor if he can't slay the dragon single-handedly. Keep your eyes and ears open for the times when you can help, when you can "dance" with him in his everyday life, when you can be proactive in your partnering.

Offer your help, or just plain pitch in. Mowing the lawn is more fun when he's mowing and you're weeding. Now you're taking care of the yard together, a shared effort that you can regard with satisfaction at the end of the day. When your chores and activities are divided, you'll see what he does and what you do. When you find opportunities for shared experiences in the ordinary activities of daily life, you will see the life you create together. What's important is that you're sharing the experience, and sharing experiences is what bonds people, joins them in that dance called "partnering."

Week #6 of Your 35 Days to a Wonderful Man: Days 26–30

This week you'll:

Involve your man in the different areas of your life.
Ask for what you want or need.
Appreciate your man's participation in your life.
Engage in your man's life.
Experience the fun of "together."

Day 26: Today I'll involve my man in the different areas of my life.

Today you'll involve your man in the different areas of your life—not just the facts of your life, but how you're thinking and feeling about the events and people of your life. Clue your man in so that he understands what's important to you, what's of interest to you right now, good or bad. Don't expect lengthy conversation; that's not the point. Let go of your fear that you won't be interesting to him if you don't keep parts of your life mysterious. Understand that if you want your man to partner you, you have to give him something to partner with. Make a list of the parts of your life you've declared off-limits to your partner. Jot down why you've kept him out. Give your man the opportunity to respect your confidence in him and treat your vulnerable areas with compassion. Today, trust him with just one of those off-limits areas. A man cannot be wonderful if he's not given anything to be wonderful about. Trust builds slowly, but it must build if you are to be genuine partners.

Day 27: Today I'll ask for what I want or need.

Today you'll bite the bullet and ask for something you want or need from your man. You won't expect him to guess what it is, and you won't blame him for not knowing already. Don't demand whatever it is, simply let him know this is what you want, this is what you would like, this is what would please you—maybe, "I don't mind doing the dishes, but I really hate emptying the dishwasher. Would you please do it for me?" or "The kids are driving me nuts. Could you please hold down the fort while I take a quick walk around the block?" Write down a list of what you have wanted from your man that you've not asked him for or only hinted at. Men are rarely good at catching hints. Now ask for one thing from that list: "Would you please sit and chat with me for a few minutes? I could really use some ideas on this thing that's bothering me." "Would you please rub my feet? I'm so achy today!" A wonderful man wants to please you; he wants to see you happy. Today, make it easy for him to do so.

Day 28: Today I'll appreciate my man's participation in my life.

Once you've opened the doors to your life to your man, he'll proffer his opinion, give you suggestions on how to do things, ask you how these things are going. You may or may not like what he has to say. Appreciate the offering either way. You're not obligated to use his feedback, just to express your gratitude for it: "Thank you, hon. I appreciate your thoughts on that." "Okay, that's a good idea. I hadn't looked at it that way. Thank you." If you do use one of his suggestions, let him know. "Your idea for how I could deal with my micromanaging boss was really good. I used it, and it worked! Thanks, hon." Your open acknowledgment and gratitude for his thoughts or efforts on your behalf nourish his desire to participate more in your life.

Observe which of your man's suggestions or ideas you shoot down, ignore, or otherwise dismiss. Today, resolve to cut that out, and turn instead to appreciating whatever he offers.

Day 29: Today I'll engage in my man's life.

Relationships are not one-way streets. For you to enjoy the benefit of your man's participation in your life, engage in his. Today, get interested in what interests him. Become a better listener. Keep up on the progress of whatever projects or hobbies he's involved in. Ask open-ended questions, such as, "So what were you able to find out about that new software you were looking at on eBay?" or "How are you thinking of putting together the cabinet you're making for so-and-so?" Listen without saying to yourself, "This is so boring—like I care about interface and downloading issues," or, sarcastically, "Angles, joints, and different glue bonding strengths—wow. Totally make my day." Say to yourself, "I am so grateful that my man is willing to engage me in his life. I enjoy supporting his enthusiasms whatever they may be." Today, engage in your man's life, if only in one area to start with. Engaging in your man's life will bring you closer together and reveal yet more of his wonderfulness to you.

Day 30: Today I'll experience the fun of "together."

You know what brought you close to your girlfriends, your sisters, your mom? Doing things together. What your most cherished memories of your near and dear ones are made of? Doing things together. Today, resolve to experience the fun of "together" with your man. Jot down what things you and your man do together and what you do apart. Next to the things you do apart, write down why you do them apart. To save time? Because you think they'd be boring to do together? Grocery shopping can be much more fun together.

Cooking together can be sensual or downright hilarious, depending on your mood. When you work out together, you can encourage each other. Make a concerted effort to do more activities together, even if that requires you to learn something new. Today, pick one and suggest it to your man. Get ready to experience the fun of "together."

Use the weekend to repeat whichever of the days were more challenging for you.

Keep track of your progress daily on your "How Did I Do Today?" chart. Enter check marks to keep track of how you did: one check for "Yes, I did," two checks for "Yes, I really did," or three for "I was brilliant on this one!" and either a minus or zero if you didn't do the item. You'll be able to see at a glance how you're doing.

Remember to keep practicing the past weeks' items as you go forward with this week's plan.

How Did I Do Today?

Days 26–30

Item	Day 26	Day 27	Day 28	Day 29	Day 30	SAT	SUN
Did I involve my man in the different areas of my life?							
Did I ask for what I want or need?							
Did I appreciate my man's participation in my life?							
Did I engage in my man's life?							
Did I experience the fun of "together"?							

Life has taught us that love does not consist in gazing at each other, but in looking outward together in the same direction.

Antoine de Saint-Exupéry

CHAPTER 7

BEST FRIENDS

A WONDERFUL MAN is your best friend.

He may not be your only best friend, but he is, most emphatically, a best friend.

A wonderful man is always on your side. A wonderful man knows all about you and loves you just the same. He knows how special and wonderful you are, and will remind you of it when you forget. A wonderful man looks out for you. He cares about what you do and who you are. A wonderful man knows what you want for yourself and will remember it for you when you're confused or lose your way.

A wonderful man is honest with you. He'll let you know when you're not being your best self, or the self you want to be, but he'll do it respectfully, offering his opinion rather than imposing his will.

Linda: My dad and Jack, my husband, have a lot of similar interests: they are both handy, they like sports and to do yard work. Their personalities, though, are very different. My dad has a quick temper, is a real type A personality. He didn't care about process but about getting things done in the most efficient way. If you made a mistake, he made you feel like a complete imbecile. As much as I was hurt by that and never want to be like that, I've also developed a type A personality; I want to get it all done now.

One time we had to change a toilet seal, and I thought we could do it ourselves, not call the plumber. Jack said, "Okay, we can do that." Well, as we changed the seal, I kept saying, "No, don't do it that way, do it this way." Finally Jack very calmly put the toilet down and said, "Linda, just listen to how you sound right now. You sound the way your father would sound. I'm not going to do the project with you if you're gonna do it like this." He called me out and made me accountable for my actions. I said, "You're absolutely right, and I don't want to be that. I don't want to be the person that I was belittled by, and even though I love my dad, that part of his personality is just not okay." Jack said, "We're on the same team here, we're trying to do this together."

We tried to fix the toilet again, and this time was fine. He helped me see that the worst that could happen is that if we did it wrong once, we'd do it again until we got it right. That's it, no big deal. I always wanted to get things right on the first try—like the whole world would crumble if I messed up once. Jack's very good at putting things in perspective, helping me see that we'll just keep going and it'll be fine. As he says, "We're on the same team." He's my best friend, I trust him, and I'm okay with that. If anything, I really appreciate it. It keeps me from becoming that totally type A personality I don't want to be.

A wonderful man will be a best friend to you and bring out the best in you as long as you let him.

Mercedes: One thing is for sure: my husband is my best friend. And we work at the same company too. We're in two different departments, but we're maybe twenty feet away from each other at all times. We literally do everything together. We have the advantage of knowing what each other has gone through in the day, so we're able to vent to each other about office situations and personalities. We choose to go to lunch together most days, and we really tend to enjoy our time together. I'd say, overall, we spend maybe 99 percent of the time together.

I don't feel like I want space. We still have the freedom to do what we want. It's not like we have to ask permission to go to lunch with someone else. I make my plans, and I let him know what they are, and vice versa. And we're never threatened. We never say, "You're going to leave. What am I going to do?" We say, "No, go ahead, I'll stay home." Or I'll say, "I'm going to go have tea with someone. Do you want to go golfing?" I encourage him to do something—not necessarily out of guilt but just to suggest something. And it's fine if he says, "No, I'd rather just hang out at home." We have the freedom to come and go like we want. It's just that mostly we want to be together.

A wonderful man is your best friend not by obligation but by desire.

Lataesha: I don't really have any specific stories about my husband being my best friend. I just know that he's mine, and I'm his! Now, of course, he doesn't take the place of the great girlfriends in my life—I need them too. But if I ever have to choose between going out with a girlfriend or my husband, I'll choose my hubby.

A wonderful man isn't an exclusive best friend, even if he is your preferred best friend.

Laurie: My husband and I were on vacation at the beach. While walking through a mall, I noticed that one my favorite stores was having a great sale. I wasn't sure I wanted to take time away from our relaxation, but Jeff encouraged me to see if there was anything I wanted to buy. We looked together, and I selected a couple of items to try on. While I was in the dressing room, one of the salesladies knocked on the door. She said, "Your husband thought this color would be beautiful on you. He asked me to bring it to you to try on." Soon she brought two or three more articles of clothing that Jeff found for me.

His patience, attention to detail, and generosity made me feel very special. I always buy more when he is with me. When I was paying for the clothing, the saleslady thanked me and said, "You can go now, but we want to keep your husband!"

A wonderful man will remind you of how special you are in many ways, large and small.

Melia: My husband is my best male friend, absolutely. Why? Because he is always there to accompany me, no matter what I want to do, and we always have fun and a great time together. If I want to see a chick flick, go shopping for shoes or clothes or groceries, whatever it is, he's there! Jorge even enjoys helping me with selections and will be totally honest when asked for his opinion. And that's the truth! Most important, when I just need to talk, when I need a really good listener, he will do just that. When I need to vent with tears about perhaps a bad day at work, problems with the kids, or just babble, he's there. It's like the lyrics to a song: "You raise me up so I can stand on mountains. You raise me up to walk on stormy seas. I am strong when I am on your shoulders."

A wonderful man cares about what you do and who you are; he's there for and with you through it all.

Lani: We often say that "we are for each other." I may do something one way and he does it another, and we'll go back and forth on it, but at some point one of us will say, "Remember, we are for each other. We're not working against each other." And that's how we remind each other we're best friends, on the same side of the fence, always there for each other.

A wonderful man is never interested in working against you, only "for" you.

Julia: My husband is my best friend. We do everything together. I have a lot of girlfriends whose husbands aren't their best friends, so I think it's kind of unusual. With Jim, I truly am his left and right arms in a lot of things that he does. Because we are so close and we love being together, we do a lot of things together. Anything he needs done, whatever he needs done, I want to help. I have no problem doing it because I want to see him fulfilled and happy in what he does, just like he wants me to be.

I have a very stressful job. I work in a busy landscape company, and it was hard for me to get time off to go on vacation because we're so busy, but my husband knew I was exhausted and just stepped in there and said, "No, we're going on vacation. You need a rest." He called my boss and told him, "I'm taking my wife away for two weeks." He just stepped in there when I couldn't, because I felt so responsible toward my job, and said, "Nope, we're gonna take time out of life for us and our relationship, and for you to rest right now." The funny part is that my boss was fine with it. He knew I'd been working really hard for a long time and didn't have a problem letting me take the time. And it was the most incredible vacation. My husband got us all packed and ready to go, and we just went! He made sure it was what I wanted to do. It was just fabulous.

A wonderful man looks out for you. He champions your best interests in word and deed.

Linda: One of the things that drew me to him at first is that he's a hunter. I love diversity. I get bored when there's nothing new in my life, so I thought, "Wow, I don't know anything about hunting, and that's really cool." I didn't try to change it. I've encouraged him. For instance, he's going next month with his brother, Brian. His brother asked him to go hunting over Labor Day weekend, and Jack said to me, "I don't think I'll go hunting with Brian because it's Labor Day weekend and what would you do?" He's always putting me first, which I really appreciate, but I said, "Go with him! How many chances do you have to go hunting with your brother?" He asked, "Are you serious? You really want me to go?" and I said, "Yes, you're gonna have fun, and we hang out enough, and we're best friends anyway, so sure, go. Have a great time."

For your wonderful man to be a best friend to you, be a best friend to him.

Laurie: I believe our hearts meet unguarded in friendship. There are safety, refuge, and security knowing that Jeff will understand me. He loves me enough to help me see another viewpoint when my perspective is clouded. If you just want someone to agree with you, you may find it difficult to truly embrace your mate as your best friend. After all, men and women are very different, and it's only when you understand and accept those differences that being best friends is possible.

Your wonderful man won't always agree with you, but he will always be a safe haven for you.

May: We get to bed about 11:00 or 12:00 at night, and I have my mind full of things I need to talk with him about: the kids, my needs, and all that. I think most men just don't like women yakking, but he is so attentive, and he will just listen. And then—like most men love to—he'll want to give me solutions. I had to say, "I don't care about your solutions, I just want you to listen to me," and he will listen, for hours at a time. He does! So instead of my spending money on a counselor or seeing a pastor, my husband listens to me. He's my confidant, my best friend. I talk to him, and I trust his opinions.

We're very different personalities, so I will ask him, "Do you think I was overreacting in this area?" and he will give me a very honest opinion. I know he always has my best interests at heart, so I can trust him a great deal. And it rubs off on my kids. In May, before Mother's Day even, my kids asked, "When is Father's Day?" They'd already picked out what they wanted to get him—cards and everything. That's how precious he is to them, and that's a reflection of the love he has put in their lives, like he has in mine.

A best friend is someone you trust. A wonderful man is a best friend you trust absolutely.

TOO OFTEN WE don't think of our mate as our best friend. Women who are with wonderful men do describe them as best friends, yet they, as Julia stated, feel that it is a rare condition, since so many of their girlfriends don't consider their husbands "best friends." We buy into the idea that the sexes are at war, which may be thrilling in the context of an affair but will become stale and hurtful through the years of a committed relationship. Indeed, one of the best predictors of a couple's satisfaction with the romance and passion in their marriage is the quality of their friendship. According to Dr. Gottman, the quality of the couple's friendship constitutes a whopping 70 percent of the determining factor of wives' satisfaction with the sex, romance, and passion in their marriage, and the figure is the same for men—70 percent! It's that friendship which is largely responsible for our intimate fulfillment, not the thrill of the chase, novel positions, or constant variety. Unfortunately, the war of the sexes precludes the deep trust that underlies a genuine friendship. It says, "We're enemies"—not to be trusted—rather than, "We're friends"—always true to each other.

A wonderful man doesn't want to be your enemy. He is on your side at all times if you will allow it. So Lani and her husband remind each other that they are "for each other," on the same team. Too often when we have disagreements with our mates, we think of ourselves as being on opposite sides instead of recognizing that we have the same goal: being happy as individuals and together. We just have different ways of getting there.

May values her husband's willingness to give her his honest opinion. She trusts that opinion, for she knows he has her best interests at heart. She can come to him with vulnerable questions like, "Do you think I overreacted?" because she knows his response will always be founded on his desire for her well-being and happiness and that he'll never use the information to hurt her. We often hesitate to approach our mates with sensitive questions, fearful that we'll somehow be giving him ammunition for a future skirmish: "You know you overreact all the time! You said it yourself!"

You can't both be locked in battle with a man and have him as a best friend. It doesn't work. Best friends look out for each other, confide in each other, hold each other's secrets, want the well-being, success, and joy of the other as much as they do their own. You can't snipe at your mate, bad-mouth him to others, spill his secrets, and laugh over his fears or vulnerabilities with your girlfriends, and then expect him to be a wonderful man, a true best friend.

When your mate is a best friend, he reveals his wonderfulness to you in special and valuable ways. For example, Julia couldn't get herself to ask for time off from work when she was clearly exhausted. Her husband stepped forward and made it possible for her to take a vacation, and then made all the arrangements so she wouldn't have any stress there either. Julia was so grateful for her husband's being a true friend to her in this way. Another woman might have said, "Wait a minute, you have no right calling my boss!" and resented the interference, not noticing the care her husband provided in so doing.

Or she might have objected to the arrangements he made, wanting to control everything rather than trust that her mate knows her well enough and is competent enough to arrange things in a pleasing manner. Not paying attention to and appreciating what our mates do on our behalf makes it difficult for them to continue behaving like a best friend.

When your mate is a best friend, he will do for you what all best friends do: call you on your "stuff" in a nonthreatening, compassionate way. When Linda slipped into behaving as her type A father would have as she and her husband were fixing a toilet, her husband pointed out her behavior so she could choose whether to continue in that vein. Linda appreciated his input—it's hard for us to see ourselves sometimes—and let him know it. She recognizes that she and her husband are always on the same team. She knows he wants only good for her and sees his comments through that lens. Most of the time when our mates call us on our bad or inappropriate behavior, all we want to do is snap back instead of reaping the benefit of his different perspective.

This brings us to the issue of trust. A best friend is, above all, someone you trust totally, implicitly, 100 percent, no holds barred. And most of us don't trust men. We expect them to lie to us, cheat on us, stomp all over our sensitivities, ignore our desires, make fun of our aspirations, and sabotage our ambitions. And since what you expect is what you get, too often that is precisely what happens. We respond with our own lies, manipulations, and seductive strategies, which further degrades any possibility of trust and, with it, any chance of genuine intimacy, true closeness, and that happily-ever-after we long for in our heart of hearts. Best friends? You're hardly friends at all at that point.

But you can't just trust any person. The truth is that not all people are trustworthy, regardless of gender. So the answer is not to trust willy-nilly, exposing your most secret, sensitive self to any man who comes along, but rather—even with a man you perceive as good—allow him to earn your trust and give him the opportunity to do so.

Earning trust can be approached as a two-step process. The first step is to take a calculated risk. When you are getting to know someone you believe is a good man, take the risk of sharing with him some small, genuinely vulnerable portion of yourself. Be sure to calculate ahead of time that if the man should betray your disclosure, the damage to you would be virtually nonexistent. For example, let him know that you had a difficult time emotionally when your cat died, and notice how he treats this disclosure. If he empathizes with you and seems sincere in appreciating what this was like for you, he's taken one step in the right direction.

Now wait a week or two and see if the man does anything detrimental with that information: gossips about you, makes derogatory remarks about people who grieve over their pets, teases you about it (it's rarely funny). If he doesn't do anything offensive, take the next calculated risk and disclose something else. Then wait and see what the man does with it. Allowing your disclosure of self to happen in small bits and slowly over time is one of the surest ways to protect yourself from an untrustworthy individual.

Step two is to observe whether the man's actions back up his words. When somebody's actions are different from his words, believe his actions. If the man you're interested in tells you that you are very important to him but every time you're to get together, he's late, then regardless of his reasons, you aren't that important to him! And much as that may sting, it is far better to evaluate correctly where you stand with someone in the first few weeks of getting to know each other than to get into a long-term relationship where you finally figure out, after having been mistreated a hundred times, that maybe you don't really matter to this person. Listen to what people say, and then watch what they do: trustworthy people back up their words with action 95 percent of the time (nobody's perfect).

When you approach developing trust safely, bit by bit, in this manner, you allow a good man to earn your trust and reveal his wonderfulness to you as he becomes that best friend wonderful men are eager to be. Trust is all-important, and it must work both ways. For your mate to reveal himself as a best friend to you, you must be a best friend to him. You must be more interested in his being the person he wants to be than you are in making or manipulating him into the person you want him to be.

So Linda, on finding out that her husband is a hunter, didn't say, "Oh, that's gross," or, "We should go bowling instead." She was open to learning about this hobby, this sport that she knew nothing about, and she didn't try to change him for any reason. If anything, Linda encouraged her husband to go hunting with his brother, even giving up her holiday weekend with him, because she knew that the hunting trip would contribute to her husband's happiness. How tempting it would have been to say, "Oh, honey, it's Labor Day, a three-day weekend! You can't just go off and spend it with your brother!" or otherwise discourage him from his hobby, with, "It's too expensive," "You're taking time away from us," or, "Why do you want to go around killing animals like some Neanderthal?"

Nurture the best friend in your man by learning about what pleases him and sharing his interest in whatever way works for you. Let your mate know you're happy to be around him, that you enjoy doing whatever together, from grocery shopping to cleaning out the garage to planning your retirement. Take the time and make the effort to get to know your mate deeply: What is his philosophy of life? What were his best and worst experiences at school? Why is a certain movie his all-time favorite film? What book or life experience moved him most deeply? Have conversations about such things, as you would with a friend. Just because you're in a committed relationship or married doesn't mean all your conversations have to be about practical matters.

Be interested in what makes your man tick, what touches him, what amuses him. Resist the urge to make fun of those things your man cherishes that you find silly or worthless. So Halloween is his favorite holiday, and he rigs up goofy haunted houses every year with his friends. So he yells back at the TV set when "his" team is messing up. So he likes to collect baseball caps he never wears. Respect what is meaningful to him; honor what he honors.

Above all, be trustworthy. Keep your promises. Follow through on what you say you will do. Show your man by your actions that he can rely on your word. Don't bad-mouth your mate to anyone, for any reason. Be loyal to him, and don't divulge his secrets or his personal idiosyncrasies. That he was busted for shoplifting at thirteen or superstitiously throws spilled salt over his left shoulder is nobody's business but yours and his.

As you show yourself to be a best friend to your mate in this way, you will bring out even more the wonderful in your man, as well as what's wonderful in you.

Week #7 of Your 35 Days to a Wonderful Man: Days 31–35

This week you'll:

Give up the battle of the sexes.
Stop bad-mouthing your man.
Quit treating your man like a child.
Be a best friend to your man.
Let your man be a best friend to you.

Day 31: Today I'll give up the battle of the sexes.

Today you'll give up the battle between the sexes. You'll realize that even though in the movies the boy and girl may fight, kiss, and live happily ever after, in real life those who see each other as enemies may occasionally kiss, but the end is rarely happy. Take stock of the ways, large or small, in which you consider your man your enemy. Are you afraid that if you tell him the truth about how you feel, he'll use it against you at some future time? Do you think that if he knows how much you've socked away from the household money to save toward that new dishwasher, he'll take it and spend it on some high-tech video game? Do you withhold sex to punish him or make him "behave"? Give it up. Today, relinquish just one of the ways you treat your man like an enemy. Tomorrow you'll let go of more.

Day 32: Today I'll stop bad-mouthing my man.

Today you'll forever put an end to bad-mouthing your man. You'll recognize that when you bad-mouth him to yourself, you lose respect for him. You erase some of that all-important ingredient to long-lasting love: admiration. When you bad-mouth your man to others, you reinforce your low opinion of him. How can true love survive in such an emotional climate? People measure up to your expectations of them. Expect your man to behave like a lowlife, and he will. Expect him to behave like the knight he wants to be, and he will do his very best to measure up. Make a list of all the ways you bad-mouth your man, and put a giant X through each of them. Right now, today, without working up to it or taking it slow, just stop bad-mouthing your man. In the end, the one who looks bad is you.

Day 33: Today I'll quit treating my man like a child.

Somewhere in the evolution of television and movies, it became okay to portray men as idiots or bumbling fools. In short order, it became okay to treat men as children. Today you'll quit doing that. Your man is not a child. A wonderful man will not accept being treated as such. You may not even realize that you've been treating your man as a child since it's so common in our culture. So sit down and make a list of all the ways you treat your man like a child. "Oh, I can't send him out for groceries; he'll forget half of what we need and come back with a ton of what we don't." "I can't ask him to plan the vacation. He'll forget about it until the last minute and make a mess of it." "His idea of cleaning is to run the vacuum cleaner a couple of times in the middle of the room." It may make you feel better, more mature, to consider your man half child, but it robs you of the wonderful partner he could be to you. Today, start treating your man like the fully functioning adult that he is. Both of you will enjoy it.

Day 34: Today I'll be a best friend to my man.

A best friend is a blessing. Today, vow to be a best friend to your man. Take a long, hard look at how you've behaved toward your man thus far. Have you been trustworthy? Have you kept his secrets? Write down the ways in which you have behaved like a true friend and the ways in which you haven't. Don't beat yourself up for whatever your failures as a friend have been. Simply, from this day forward, be a worthy friend. Don't divulge his vulnerabilities, lack of success, or mistakes to others. Don't go behind his back (unless it's to plan that terrific surprise party for him!). Make his interests as important to you as your own. Without hesitation or reluctance, from now on be a best friend to your man. The rewards will be great.

Day 35: Today I'll let my man be a best friend to me.

You trust a best friend to do right by you—not to do or say anything that isn't in your best interests. Today, allow your man to be that best friend to you. Refrain from hearing what he says to you with suspicion: "What does he want now?" "Why is he saying this?" Appreciate his feedback and input for what it is: a desire to contribute to your well-being. It may take a while for you to trust him as you do your best girlfriend. That's all right. But start now. Today, deliberately accept what he says to you as coming from a friend whose only concern is for you to be happy. Today, when he does something for you, even if he doesn't do it in exactly the way you would have done it yourself, accept and appreciate his effort as that of a best friend. Your world will be enriched, and your love will be the stronger for it.

Use the weekend to repeat whichever of the days were more challenging for you.

Keep track of your progress daily on your "How Did I Do Today?" chart. Enter check marks to keep track of how you did: one check for "Yes, I did," two checks for "Yes, I really did," or three for "I was brilliant on this one!" and either a minus or zero if you didn't do the item. You'll be able to see at a glance how you're doing.

Remember to keep practicing the past weeks' items as you go forward with this week's plan.

How Did I Do Today?

Days 31–35

Item	Day 31	Day 32	Day 33	Day 34	Day 35	SAT	SUN
Did I give up the battle of the sexes?							
Did I stop bad-mouthing my man?							
Did I quit treating my man like a child?							
Was I a best friend to my man?							
Did I let my man be a best friend to me?							

My best friend is the one who brings out the best in me.

Henry Ford

CHAPTER 8

KEEPING IT WONDERFUL

C ONGRATULATIONS! Now that you've completed your 35-day plan, whether it took you 35 days or 365, you have revealed much of what is wonderful in your man. As you continue to work with whatever items were most challenging for you, you will reveal even more of his wonderfulness and enjoy a far richer, deeper, and more satisfying relationship. You will also find that you have grown as a person, and that all your other relationships will benefit from all that you have discovered about yourself.

The more you value the differences between you, the more you value your own uniqueness; the more you praise your man, the more you learn to esteem value—your own as well as his. The more you accept your man as he is, the more you learn to accept yourself as you are. The more you encourage your man to live his dream, the more you'll be able to encourage yourself to live yours. You cannot forgive another fully without forgiving yourself. As you engage in your man's life, you encourage him to engage in yours, and it's never a one-way street being best friends. As you support the wonderfulness in your man, you can't help but support it in yourself as well.

As you do so, you make it possible for your man to see how wonderful you are. Cherish that. He becomes inspired, motivated, to be your prince now that you are treating him as such. He treats you as his princess, his queen, in return. Nowhere is it more true that like attracts like than in the realm of relationships. People who like very different things are certainly attracted to each other. The point is that like attracts like in the dynamic energy of a relationship. The Ladies' stories make this point clear. It is not the differences between us but how we view those differences that makes for joy or despair.

Commit to discover and nurture the wonderfulness in your man, reveal your own wonderfulness in the process, and you will create a continuous upward spiral of mutual love and respect that can lead to what we so ardently desire in our heart of hearts: true and lasting love, that blissful heaven on earth.

MEN TO AVOID

MOST MEN ARE GOOD GUYS. When they show the characteristics described in Chapter 1, they can reveal their wonderfulness readily. There is really only one main category of man who just won't fit into the good guy category when it comes to relationships, and that's the abusive individual. Abusive individuals vary tremendously in terms of looks, occupations, ages, personality, ethnic backgrounds, wealth, and so on. What they have in common is a behavioral style predicated on power and control: their attempt to assert power over you and control you. The easiest way to help you know what men to avoid in your search for a good man is to describe that behavioral style in a series of warning signs. You will find these elaborated in far greater detail in my book, *Dangerous Relationships: How to Identify and Respond to the Seven Warning Signs of a Troubled Relationship.*

Warning Sign #1: A Whirlwind Beginning

Whether romantic, sexual, or platonic, the beginning of an abusive relationship is typically intense. There's often a feeling of hot pursuit, where partners of abusers find themselves vigorously pursued by the abuser. The pursuit is marked by charm, passion, huge amounts of attention, compliments, and gifts. Victims—although they certainly don't appear to be victims at this point—feel as if they are the most important thing in the abuser's life. They are made to feel incredibly special, wanted, and appreciated.

So what's the problem? What is wrong with being lavished with attention and affection? What is wrong with being cared about? Nothing, of course. Many wonderful marriages, friendships, and love affairs are based on such feelings. Many nonabusive cults and sects provide such feelings for their members. The problem is that sometime in this wonderful beginning, abusers will pressure their partner to do something that is uncomfortable for her without regard for her discomfort.

For example, abusers may want to have sex before the pursued individual is ready, or want to see the object of their desire far more than desired by their partner. Abusers may want to move in together right away. When their partners protest, abusers ignore their protestations and pressure with more flattery, attention, and words of love. Flooded with good feelings, the pursued individuals will override their discomfort and go along with the abuser's desire. These individuals dismiss their feeling of being bulldozed into doing something they didn't really want to do. They ignore the long-term implications of not doing what's right for them in order to please the abuser.

The danger of a whirlwind beginning is not the whirlwind of attention in and of itself, but how abusers profit from the "high" that this attention gives their partner: It gives them the power to pressure their partner into doing something she doesn't want to do. Since the pressure takes the form of nice words and dulcet tones, individuals allow it. They don't realize that this is but the beginning of an underlying dynamic: the profound disregard abusers of all types have for the rights and feelings of others.

Warning Sign #2: Possessiveness

Abusive relationships are about power and control—the power of the abusers over the individuals they are involved with. Abusers don't see their partners as separate beings, with their own identity, rights, hopes, and dreams. Abusers see their partners as possessions, things that belong to them and exist for the sole purpose of pleasing them.

How do the early signs of this possessiveness manifest themselves? In the beginning, abusers seek to control their partners' time, whom they see, and under what circumstances. For example, abusers will either want to be with their partners all the time or insist that their partners be available to them whenever they desire. They explain their interest in togetherness and exclusivity with "Because I love you so much," and their partners will feel flattered and acquiesce. Abusers will say that they want to know where the partner is going, what the partner is doing, and who with throughout the day: "Because I worry about you, I want to keep you safe." Partners, flattered by someone's caring that much, won't initially think about the controlling aspect of such behavior. To feel so wanted is very compelling.

As abusers are subtly controlling their victim's time, they are systematically excluding other individuals from that person's life. This is one of the most insidious and powerful ways in which control initially operates.

Abusers, for example, will denigrate their partners' friends or family, saying things like, "They're not good enough for you," "They don't really care about you like I do," or "They're never there for you, they just take from you," to discourage the partner from wanting to spend time with friends and family. Abusers will also imply, "I'm all you need" and "I'm the only one who really cares for you," which, when the partner is in the throes of the whirlwind beginning, seems true.

By systematically excluding all familiar support systems, abusers cut partners off from their normal sources of feedback and reality checks. In the absence of these sources, partners have no way of gaining perspective on their current experience and are deprived of alternate points of view. Partners are then truly isolated and alone, with no one to turn to for understanding, comfort, and love—except to the abuser. Now the abuser is truly in control.

As the relationship with an abuser continues, the partner's life becomes increasingly restricted. The longer the relationship goes on, the more control abusers exercise. Eventually an abuser will dictate everything the partner may or may not do, from major decisions such as where to work and live, to what happens to the partner's money, body, and possessions, to choices such as what clothes to wear and food to eat.

Interestingly enough, abusers justify their right to run the partner's life on the basis of their love and caring for the partner. "It's for your own good" or "for the good of the relationship/cult," they'll say. Abusers will convince their partners that their dislike of the partner's friends is based on worldly wisdom, a deeper knowledge of people, and that they are thus protecting the partner from harm—all in the partner's best interests.

This approach is often difficult for partners to resist, because it doesn't seem to be manipulation. It just seems like someone appealing to their rational mind, helping them see something that they should have realized was good for them in the first place.

Warning Sign #3: The Switch

At some point early in the relationship, the partner will say or do something to which the abuser will have an extreme reaction. For example, the partner will be a few minutes late to an appointment, and the abuser will scream or turn to ice for days. The partner becomes completely disoriented. The difference between the loving, caring, gentle person an abuser was before the incident and the screaming maniac the partner is now faced with makes no sense. The partner is right: the abuser's switch makes sense only relative to how the abuser defined the event, which is usually impossible for the partner to know. Abusers are not interested in their partner's explanations of why a particular behavior occurred and are unwilling to discuss their reactions. Abusers expect their partners to accept that they are justified in their extreme reaction.

Warning Sign #4: Blame

Abusers consistently blame others for whatever goes wrong in their world. Abusers also blame others for their unhappy feelings and their inappropriate behavior. Even if at some later point abusers express remorse, they do not take responsibility for their behavior. Regardless of the circumstances, it is always somebody else's fault if abusers feel unhappy or angry. Abusers will, for example, blame their partners if they had a bad day at work, a rotten time in traffic, got fired, have an ingrown toenail, or failed to win the lottery. The obvious lack of rational connection between their partner's behavior and the abuser's life events is irrelevant. To an abuser, whatever goes wrong is the partner's fault.

Abusers also blame their partners for the partner's unhappiness. If, for example, the partner expresses loneliness because the abuser is out every night, the abuser will blame the partner for being "no fun" and therefore causing the abuser's nightly absence. Abusers thus absolve themselves of all responsibility. There is no compassion for the partner's feelings, sharing of responsibility, or even discussion of possible shared responsibility. Whatever goes wrong in the partner's life is fully the partner's responsibility.

Individuals in abusive relationships don't want their dream to come crashing down. They don't want to believe that the abuser, who was so loving and attentive at the beginning of the relationship, could possibly also be cruel, irrational, and unloving. That's just too painful. So when abusers tells their partners, for example, that they are upset and it is their partner's fault, the partner is only too willing to accept the blame.

Warning Sign #5: Verbal Abuse

In the development of a violent domestic or dating relationship, there is a predictable sequence: the physical violence that is to come later in the relationship is always preceded by other types of hurtful behaviors. The most common is verbal abuse. Verbal abuse comes in all shapes and sizes, from the most easily recognizable insults of the "bitch/bastard" variety to indirect criticisms, general negativity, and demeaning put-downs. Abusers are verbally abusive without regard to the pain it causes. They are as free with cutting words as they will later be with fists and kicks.

Warning Sign #6: Insensitivity

Long before abusers engage in violence toward their partner, their disposition to do so shows up in other areas. Most often, abusers show their true colors as they willfully neglect the well-being of children, animals, and plants. They disregard or destroy the property of others. Abusers generally have no concern for the pain and suffering in the world, even in their immediate world. If, for example, a partner's parent is ailing and the partner wants to visit the parent in the hospital, the abuser will say, "What for? Doesn't your parent have a doctor?" and be aggravated by the partner's wish. If, for example, abusers acquire a pet, they will usually lose interest in the animal after a brief initial infatuation and fail to attend to the animal's needs, oblivious to and usually annoyed by the animal's obviously failing condition.

This warning sign is one of the most telling. No matter how much they cherish you in the beginning, people who can ignore the suffering of those around them—whether they cause the suffering or not—will eventually ignore yours.

Warning Sign #7: Past and Present Violence

To abusers, violence is an acceptable response to stress and frustration. Violence is part of the larger pattern of power and control over others as the primary way of interacting with a partner. The use of force or any display of physical violence toward a partner in a relationship is the single most reliable predictor of a violent domestic or dating relationship.

Physical violence in abusive relationships can be direct or indirect. Direct is hands-on force: shoving, hitting, pinning down, pulling or pushing a body part, and kicking. Indirect violence does not involve laying a hand on the individual: throwing objects, tearing up a room, kicking objects, walking a person into a wall or other dangerous area, locking a person in or confining a person to a room or area, or depriving a person of sleep, food, water, or other essentials. Both kinds of violence are usually used in combination with threats of future or further violence. Many individuals fail to recognize indirect physical violence for the physical force that it is.

Even if they do recognize the use of physical force, individuals in an abusive relationship are rarely willing to see the violence for what it is. They collude with the abuser in whitewashing the violence, thus giving tacit permission to continue the abuse. Individuals don't do this because they are stupid or masochistic; they collude in minimizing the abuse because the horror of what is happening to them is too great to bear.

One of the most wonderful things about a close relationship with a person or a group is the feeling of safety inherent in the relationship. Given the precarious nature of the world we live in, such a relationship often provides the only place people feel truly safe and secure.

When abusers do something to shatter the safety, the partner is in shock. She doesn't want to believe it is happening. The partner doesn't want to admit, especially not to herself, that the safe haven she thought she found is a sham—that loving this person means being hurt, and that whatever the abuser calls "caring" doesn't include caring about the partner's well-being.

The partner wants the fairytale back—those wonderful three months or so at the beginning of the relationship when it all felt so magical. So the partner will deny and discount the violence, hoping to make it all go away, and will never really address the source of the violence or deal with it realistically.

The partner will seek to rationalize the behavior and come up with "reasons" to make the unacceptable acceptable. Partners, for example, will rationalize the abuser's throwing things at them as an understandable, although painful, response to a stressful day at work. They deny the obvious: that throwing things is never an acceptable way to deal with any problem.

Another way partners attempt to make the violence go away is to discount it—make it appear less violent and less hurtful than it really is: "Well, my partner didn't hit me, so it wasn't violence." In many instances, victims of domestic violence discount anything short of outright battering.

Past violence is the surest predicator of future violence. When people hear of violence toward someone else, they often think, "Oh, that could never happen to me. The other person must have done something awful to deserve that. My partner would never be violent like that." Not so. Although people certainly can and do change, past violence remains the number one predictor of future violence. Just as callousness toward the suffering of others will eventually become callousness toward the partner, so too will violence toward others eventually become violence toward the partner.

Those are the seven warning signs. Forewarned is, as always, forearmed. I hope you'll never run into an abusive individual on your way to a wonderful man, but if you do, step aside, for there are many genuinely good men out there eager to be your wonderful man.

RECOMMENDED READING

Babcock, Linda, and Laschever, Sara. *Women Don't Ask*. Princeton, NJ: Princeton University Press, 2003.

Baumeister, Roy F. *The Cultural Animal*. New York: Oxford University Press, 2005.

Chapman, Gary. *The Five Love Languages*. Chicago: Northfield Publishing, 1995.

Goleman, Daniel. *Emotional Intelligence*. New York: Bantam Books, 1995.

Gottman, John. *Why Marriages Succeed or Fail*. New York: Fireside, 1994.

Gottman, John, and Silver, Nan. *The Seven Principles for Making Marriage Work*. New York: Three Rivers Press, 1999.

Gray, John. *Men Are from Mars, Women Are from Venus*. New York: HarperCollins, 1995.

Langer, Ellen J. *Mindfulness*. New York: Perseus, 1989.

Nelson, Noelle. *Dangerous Relationships*. New York: Perseus, 2001.

Schulz, Mona Lisa. *The New Feminine Brain*. New York: Free Press, 2005.

Seligman, Martin E. P. *Learned Optimism*. New York: Pocket Books, 1998.

Tannen, Deborah. *You Just Don't Understand*. New York: William Morrow, 1990.

ACKNOWLEDGMENTS

THIS BOOK WOULD NOT have been possible without the lively participation of the Ladies, that incomparable group of women who shared so freely and honestly the stories of their relationships, and all that I have learned from my clients over the years. To them I say "thank you" with all my heart and then some. I am deeply grateful to my agent, Dena Fischer, for having faith in my work and helping me, with grace, patience, and unfailing good humor, to step up to the next level in my writing career. I am thankful to everyone at Free Press, without whose passionate commitment and terrific efforts this book would still be just another file on my computer. My profound thanks to my editor, Leslie Meredith, and her assistant, Donna Loffredo, whose insightful comments and professional wisdom corralled my wayward words into a finished piece worthy of my beloved readers. I am also very appreciative of the fine work my publicist, Jill Browning, and her department at Free Press did on my behalf. As always, special thanks go to Diane Rumbaugh and Michelle Masamitsu, as well as to my friends and family. For everything you are and do, I am immensely grateful.

ABOUT THE AUTHOR

NOELLE C. NELSON, Ph.D., is a psychologist, popular seminar leader, speaker, and author of nine books, including *Dangerous Relationships: How to Identify and Respond to the Seven Warning Signs of a Troubled Relationship* and *The Power of Appreciation: The Key to a Vibrant Life*. Through the years, her work has empowered countless individuals to be happier, healthier, and more successful at work, at home, and in relationships.

Born in Manhattan to a French mother and an American father, Dr. Nelson lives in southern California. Her hobbies include reading everything from mysteries to historical fiction, enjoying Latin jazz, and snorkeling wherever warm waters are to be found. Visit her website at www.yourmaniswonderful.com.